C000140910

CHURCHES OF GLASGOW

GORDON ADAMS

AMBERLEY

For Alice and Anna
&
Gary for his contributions to the book, proof reading and patience.

This edition first published 2021

Amberley Publishing
The Hill, Stroud
Gloucestershire GL5 4EP

www.amberley-books.com

Copyright © Gordon Adams, 2021

The right of Gordon Adams to be identified as the Author
of this work has been asserted in accordance with the
Copyrights, Designs and Patents Act 1988.

All rights reserved. No part of this book may be reprinted
or reproduced or utilised in any form or by any electronic,
mechanical or other means, now known or hereafter invented, including
photocopying and recording, or in any information
storage or retrieval system, without the permission in writing
from the Publishers.

British Library Cataloguing in Publication Data.
A catalogue record for this book is available from the British Library.

ISBN 978 1 3981 0432 7 (print)
ISBN 978 1 3981 0433 4 (ebook)

Typesetting by SJmagic DESIGN SERVICES, India.
Printed in Great Britain.

CONTENTS

INTRODUCTION

The intention of this book is to highlight the variety of places of worship throughout Glasgow. It includes some of the most iconic buildings, some of the less well known and a few of the ruined, dilapidated and forgotten. Each one has its own story and they all form part of the heritage of religious history and architecture which enrich the city.

St Andrew is the patron saint of Scotland while St Kentigern – more commonly recognised by Glaswegians as St Mungo – is the patron saint of Glasgow. Both saints are well represented throughout the city's churches. The city's coat of arms represents its saint with the abbreviated motto of 'Let Glasgow Flourish' with a representation of four miracles attributed to St Mungo in the form of a tree, bird, bell and fish with a ring in its mouth. These are included in a rhyme that children often learn along the lines of 'This is the tree that never grew, this is the bird that never flew, this is the bell that never rang and this is the fish that never swam.' A fuller city motto is 'Lord, let Glasgow flourish through the preaching of thy word and praising thy name.' This is believed to have first appeared on a bell made for Glasgow's Tron St Mary's Church in 1631.

Until fairly recent times, the influence of religious bodies used to be more pervasive and directive in the life of Glaswegians, whether for good or bad depending on your own beliefs. The range of those religious bodies was predominantly restricted to Roman Catholicism, Episcopalianism and various Protestant/Presbyterian belief systems. As a child in the 1950s, living in the Bridgeton district of Glasgow, there seemed to be churches all over the place with small gospel halls in the most surprising of locations. My primary school was built for the Bridgeton Free Church and I attended Sunday school at Bridgeton & Newhall Parish Church of Scotland. I even have vague recollections of attending Magic Lantern shows in the local Bethany Hall.

Some of my friends attended the Roman Catholic Sacred Heart chapel facing directly over to my church, seeming almost to confront each other. Others didn't identify with any religion. There was no real sense of religious animosity between us but I do recall being jealous of some friends who were lucky enough to be in the Scouts (neutral) and who always seemed to be involved in various adventures. I was in the Lifeboys (Protestant) and I mostly recall marching relentlessly about a church hall. Fortunately, the notorious days of the gangs had passed and the Norman Conks (Catholic) and the Bridgeton Billy Boys (Protestant) no longer existed to contest for territory. I certainly do not recall engaging in any religious war with my own friends.

I had left the district behind when I moved to Auchenshuggle (yes, it does exist) in 1967, but by the mid-1970s I began to notice that my previous stomping ground was rapidly being demolished. I decided to undertake a photographic record of Bridgeton, Calton and Dalmarnock before they were gone forever. It was during this effort that I became more aware of the large number of places of worship in these localities and that they were not all simply Roman Catholic or Church of Scotland. I also developed a clearer understanding of the historical development of the various religions and how they had interacted with each other and moulded the very country that I lived in as well as myself.

From that experience and further study, I have come to recognise that in order to understand the history of Scotland and the society it has produced, it is necessary to understand at least the basics of this country's religious history. Over the centuries religion has been the source of great strife and hardship within Scotland and has resulted in significant wars, especially with England. It resulted in the invasion of Scotland by Oliver Cromwell during the Civil War that affected all of the UK's countries in the mid-seventeenth century. It was instrumental in precipitating the Act of Union of 1707 between Scotland and England and the subsequent Jacobite rebellions. However, it also resulted in a countrywide policy of compulsory education in Scotland which helped facilitate the Age of Enlightenment and the Industrial Revolution.

This book touches only lightly on the remarkable variation in religions which now enrich the culture of the city but I hope it is enough to spark a further interest in the reader since these matters still affect us all to some degree. If nothing else, I hope you enjoy the variety of architecture which still graces the landscape of the city, from the simple, small and circumspect places of worship to the huge, grand and imposing. That said, I have tried not to include too much architectural description of the buildings – you don't need to know this to decide if you enjoy their appearance or not. Also, even a small book such as this contains a significant amount of factual information and errors can creep in. So, my apologies in advance if this has happened. It is surprising how many variations of the same factual information are out there!

Finally, this book has mostly been produced during the Covid-19 pandemic with places of worship closed to reduce the spread of the virus. Given the numerous difficulties arising during this period I wish to thank everyone who was able to contribute to the compilation of this book and help facilitate its publication at a very testing and highly unusual time.

Gordon Adams,
14 July, 2020

SOME INFORMATION
All buildings in the book are listed alphabetically by their current usage, for example Tron Theatre, followed by its last religious usage – Tron St Mary's. If it is currently in use as a place of worship, that is the only name listed. Where a building currently has no name, its final religious designation is used.

Some useful dates:

1843 – The Disruption = Free Church established
1900 – Union of United Presbyterian (UP) and Free Churches = United Free (UF)
1929 – Union of UF and Church of Scotland = Church of Scotland

1. ADELAIDE PLACE BAPTIST CHURCH
209 Bath St., City Centre, G2 4HZ

Above: Adelaide Place and its interior – one of Glasgow's many Greek Temples.

Adelaide Place was built in 1875–77. The general design was a very popular one in Glasgow of the period; a 'Greek temple' believed to have been influenced by Alexander 'Greek' Thomson. The congregation continues to thrive today and uses the space for several purposes which include a pre-school nursery, venue spaces and a small guest house. An earlier 'chapel' is recorded as having opened in Hope St on 13 September 1835 but there appears to have been activity prior to this date. The church magazine of July/August 1959 provides a few examples of why people might have been cut off from the congregation in earlier days:

- James C: Cut off 20 June 1830 for betting about a prize fight in England.
- Thomas D: Cut off 27 February 1831 for idleness, lying and evil speaking.
- Jean M: Cut off 18 December 1839 for disobedience and insubordination to her Mistress.

2. AL FAROOQ MOSQUE, EDUCATION & COMMUNITY CENTRE
34 Dixon St., Crosshill, G42 8EJ

The Al Farooq Mosque in Crosshill is an example of a notable building which can effectively be repurposed rather than demolished. It was built in 1893 for the Crosshill Free Church which ended its days as Crosshill Victoria Church of Scotland in 1972. The mosque opened in the late 1990s.

The Baillieston Church is now private property but the graveyard remains accessible.

3. BAILLIESTON ST ANDREW'S PARISH CHURCH OF SCOTLAND
50 Church St., Baillieston, G69 7EX

At the turn of the nineteenth century what is now known as Baillieston was a collection of small hamlets. On Crosshill Farm a Church of Scotland chapel of ease – Crosshill Chapel – was erected in 1833. It was, and remains, a simple building with a graveyard added in 1840. Sadly, the graveyard would soon be used for the victims of a cholera epidemic. It eventually took the name Baillieston St Andrew's when Rhinsdale Church's congregation joined it in 1966. Sometime after this it was found that the church had quite serious problems and it was decided that a new one should be built. The outcome was a new Baillieston St Andrew's in Bredisholme Road which opened in 1974. The old church was saved when it was converted into a house.

4. BARLANARK GREYFRIARS CHURCH OF SCOTLAND
365 Hallhill Rd, Barlanark, G33 4RY

In the Inquisition of Prince David of 1116 Barlanark was recorded as having been an extensive possession of Glasgow Cathedral at one time. After his enquiry it was restored to the cathedral. It became a prebend of the medieval cathedral, a prebend being a portion of the cathedral lands allocated to an important member of the clergy to support him and his activities. It is hugely unlikely, but the town and country houses of the prebend of Barlanark have both survived with the Provand's Lordship in Townhead (the oldest house in Glasgow) and Provan Hall in Auchinlea Park, Easterhouse.

Barlanark Greyfriars was built to serve a huge influx of people to the area.

Barlanark was home to one of the earlier post-Second World War housing schemes built by Glasgow. From 1952–53 more than 2,300 'Corporation' houses became available for renting out. With this major influx of people to the area a church extension was deemed necessary. The Barlanark church started in 1954 with a minister and a wooden hut, but by 1956 a building was dedicated as Barlanark & Wellhouse Church, financed by the Women's Guild. This was a hall-church and it was not until 1970 that the present sanctuary was completed. It was also in this year that the church renamed itself as Barlanark Greyfriars in thanks for the gift of the money received from the sale of the Greyfriars & Alexandra Parade Church building following the dissolution of that congregation.

5. Barony Hall/Barony Ramshorn Church of Scotland
1 MacLeod St., Townhead, G4 0RA

The 1560 Protestant Scottish Reformation resulted in the national disestablishment of the Catholic Church. By the end of the sixth century however, it was acknowledged that the extensive rural area of the new Protestant Glasgow Parish could no longer be provided for effectively. Therefore, the extensive area north of the Clyde from Partick in the west to Lochwood in the east, and north to Bishopbriggs was again disjoined from Glasgow Parish as the Barony Parish in 1595. It took its title from the ancient feudal patrimony of the Catholic See of Glasgow – the Barony of Glasgow.

The Barony Church was established in the crypt of the cathedral where the congregation spent the next 204 years in this unlikely and inhospitable location.

The Barony Parish was one of the oldest of the Church of Scotland.

With the opening of a new Barony church beside the cathedral in 1799 the crypt was used as a burial ground. In later years one of its ministers, Dr Norman McLeod, is said to have informed Queen Victoria that it was 'the ugliest Kirk in all Europe'.

With the tremendous growth in population in subsequent years the Barony found itself subject to the same pressures that Glasgow Parish had experienced. To address the problem chapels of ease – churches with limited authority – were built throughout the Barony. These proved so successful that four chapels were later separated off as independent parishes – Shettleston (1847), Calton (1849), Maryhill (1850) and Springburn (1854) – and within each of these other parishes gradually developed to meet the needs of the population.

When a new building was eventually needed again a magnificent, red-sandstone church was raised in Castle Street in 1889. It provided a superb home for the congregation, and was later joined by a number of other congregations. As Barony Ramshorn, its last service was held on 6 October, 1985. A Barony chapel was opened in the cathedral crypt and some parishioners returned there. The building was acquired by Strathclyde University in 1986 and was named Barony Hall. The Barony parish was in existence for 390 years and was one of the most important parishes of the Church of Scotland.

6. Bridgeton Baptist Church
82 Orr St., Bridgeton, G40 2QF

Situated within the district of Mile-end, near its boundary with Bridgeton Cross, is the red-sandstone Baptist Church. The original congregation, the Church of

A 1906 'Academy Architecture' illustration of this building's original details.

Christ, arrived in Bridgeton from Rutherglen in 1870 and moved to a number of locations in the area in the following years. A majority of the congregation eventually joined the Baptist Union in 1879 as Canning Street Baptist Church (Canning Street now being part of the present London Road at the Cross).

In 1883 the original St Clement's Church of Scotland in Orr Street was purchased by the Baptists. It was used for a time then replaced by a new building in 1906. With the ongoing loss of the local population to the new peripheral housing estates the church closed in 1967. The building was acquired by Andrew Watt Car Parts and used as a warehouse until 2012, which helped ensure that the building survived the wholesale demolition which took place during the Glasgow Eastern Area Renewal Project (GEAR) of the 1970s. At this time, its current usage is not known.

7. BRIDGETON ST FRANCIS IN THE EAST CHURCH OF SCOTLAND
26 Queen Mary St., Bridgeton, G40 3BB

Barrowfield Parish Church of Scotland was built in 1873 and took its name from the old estate of Barrowfield on which it and Bridgeton were built. The church thrived in a heyday of church attendance, but it also shared in the general decline which was to follow. By 1929 the congregation numbered a mere thirteen, the building was deteriorating rapidly, gas and water supplies were cut off and there was no minister.

Barrowfield was saved by the intervention of the Reverend Sydney Warnes of St Mary's, Partick, who declared that the Church of Scotland could not abandon a district such as Bridgeton which was so very much in need of spiritual and material sustenance. Warnes put his beliefs into practice and was inducted as the minister in January 1930. On his first visit the story goes that he was escorted to the church from Bridgeton Cross station by a posse of the notorious Billy Boys

Above left: The remarkably resilient St Francis in the East.

Above right: The *Rise Up and Build* mural.

who felt he needed protection. Repairs and restructuring were undertaken and the revived church took a new name – St Francis in the East. In 1955 as part of the church's silver jubilee celebrations a mural, *Rise Up and Build*, was painted behind the communion table by the artist Walter Pritchard and students from the Glasgow Art School. The initial sketch was by Alasdair Gray. The mural depicts St Francis rebuilding the church of St Damian in Assisi on the left, fusing into the building of St Francis in the East on the right.

In the 1970s, with the massive Glasgow Eastern Area Renewal Project (GEAR), Bridgeton lost most of its housing and population. At one point almost the whole area around the church was empty of houses and former parishioners would travel from their new housing schemes to keep the church going. In 1986 the prefix of Bridgeton was added to the church's designation to mark its union with Bridgeton Parish Church's congregation. The story of the church's survival and its support for its community is inspiring. Two books have been written about it – John Sim's 1955 *A Light in Bridgeton* and Bill Shackleton's 2005 *Keeping it Cheery: Anecdotes from a Life in Brigton*.

8. Burnside Blairbeth Parish Church of Scotland
2 Church Ave, Burnside, Rutherglen, G73 5BX

This church is not in Glasgow, it is in Rutherglen, and so it should not be in this book. The justification for its inclusion is its extraordinary story – it used to be in Glasgow. Burnside Blairbeth started as a mission named St Gilbert's in 1903 in a temporary iron church in Pollokshields. A permanent home was built in 1909–11. There came a point in 1942 when the congregation was united with that of Sherbrooke Church of Scotland and the St Gilbert's building lay empty and became surplus to requirements.

Meanwhile, a congregation in Rutherglen had been using a church hall since 1928 and plans for a new building had been thwarted by the coming of the

Burnside
Blairbeth –
a moveable
church!

Second World War. From 1947 however it began negotiating for the purchase of St Gilbert's and succeeded. St Gilbert's was then taken down and removed stone by stone to Rutherglen between 1950–54 and rebuilt at its present site as Burnside Parish Church of Scotland. In 2002 it was joined by the congregation of Blairbeth Rodger Memorial to become Burnside Blairbeth.

9. CALEDONIA ROAD UP CHURCH
1 Caledonia Rd, Gorbals, G5 9DP

The origin of this church lies in 1799 when the congregation of the Hutchesontown Relief Church was established in the Gorbals, and later became a United Presbyterian congregation.

By 1854, some members of Hutchesontown appear to have become unhappy with their church for some reason and sought to have a new one built. The majority disagreed, so the disaffected group broke away to fulfil its ambition. This was achieved when the Caledonia Road UP building was opened in 1857. The new church was the first of four churches built in Glasgow by the celebrated Alexander 'Greek' Thomson.

In 1900 both the original and the new church participated in the union of the UP and Free Churches to form the United Free Church. Hutchesontown was eventually terminated in 1924 with the remaining members joining Caledonia Road, with the latter renaming itself as Hutchesontown & Caledonia Road. Its life as a church ended in 1963 and was sold to what was then Glasgow Corporation. Sadly, the building was vandalised and then badly damaged in a fire in 1965. The exterior was saved however and was partially restored given its importance. It remains a site frequented by architectural aficionados and tourists, drawn by the reputation of Thomson. The church is now routinely referred to by its original title of Caledonia Road UP Church.

The Gorbals was a densely populated district before many people were moved out to housing estates by the city authorities as part of slum clearances. The church now sits on a traffic island, effectively isolated by busy roads and surrounded by a sparsely

Caledonian Road – Alexander 'Greek' Thomson's first Glasgow church.

populated area. It is now one of the few survivors of nineteenth-century architecture in the district and currently remains in the ownership of Glasgow City Council.

10. CALTON PARKHEAD CHURCH OF SCOTLAND
122 Helenvale St, Parkhead, G31 4NA

Established in 1793 at 27 Tobago Street, Calton was among the first chapels of ease opened to alleviate pressure on the limited resources of the Barony Parish. The parish eventually allocated to the Calton church reached as far east as Parkhead. In the early 1930s, to combat the appalling housing conditions in Calton, many of the inhabitants were removed to new Corporation housing built in the Newbank, Cuthelton and Lilybank areas. The church, then Calton Old, followed its congregation.

A small mission church had already been built in Helenvale Street in 1905, Calton East Church, but it was replaced by a new building to accommodate both Calton East

Calton Parkhead – an Early Christian/Byzantine church in the east end.

Calton Parkhead
Church's interior.

and Calton Old. The building was named Calton Old (Newbank) Church and was
opened in 1935. It acquired its current name when joined by the congregations of both
Parkhead and Dalmarnock Churches in 1977. A feature in the vestibule of the church
is the hour hand of a clock in the shape of a Celtic Cross, acquired by a minister from
the landmark Boots store in the city centre when it was being demolished.

11. CATHCART OLD PARISH (ST OSWALD'S) CHURCH OF SCOTLAND
119 Carmunnock Rd, Cathcart, G44 5UW

Cathcart is a very old site of religious activity. Its first recorded building however –
'a plain barn-like structure' – was built in 1707 and used until 1831. Cathcart
Old's present church, the third, was completed in 1928.

From the west, in
the wintry light,
the tower gives a
good impression
of an impregnable
fortress with
its feudal lord's
banner flying.

The ruins in the old
graveyard – the tower and
the belfry – are those of the
1831–1928 church.

A commemorative booklet produced in 1979 by Jean Marshall marked the 800th anniversary of the parish. It also outlined some possible evidence of an even earlier origin, taking the history beyond the ninth century AD to St Oswald (*c*. AD 604–*c*. AD 642). Oswald, to whom the Cathcart church is dedicated, was converted to Christianity at Iona and later became King of Northumbria. With the subsequent growth of Catholicism and its antagonism towards the Celtic church, of which Oswald was a part, dedications to him were not usually made after the early ninth century. It is suggested therefore that a religious centre at Cathcart in the name of St Oswald may actually pre-date the early ninth century, taking the church's history back by another 300 years at least.

Cathcart's churchyard is still in use but is no longer routinely accessible due to the potential dangers from the ruins there. Its closure helps to prevent acts of vandalism against the monuments, some of which are of historical significance. One of the better-known gravestones is the Polmadie Martyrs' Memorial, marking the grave of three men executed in 1685 in the Covenanting years.

Whether or not the church has a connection with St Oswald which pushes its history further back, 841 years in itself is remarkable.

12. CATHEDRAL CHURCH OF ST MUNGO
Cathedral Precinct, Castle St, Townhead, G4 0QZ

The story of St Kentigern, or St Mungo as he is better known in Glasgow, has it that when the Romans still occupied Britain St Ninian passed through the settlement of Cathures (or Gleschu) on the west bank of the Molendinar burn in the late fourth century and consecrated a cemetery there. Around 200 years later St Mungo was travelling to the west from Culross and met a holy man named Fergus who was dying. When Fergus died St Mungo buried him in St Ninian's cemetery and founded a religious community before he departed. He returned in 581 where he died in 603. At some point the location became known as Glasgow.

The religious community appears to have lapsed into obscurity until Prince David, later King David I, compiled his Inquisition of 1116 into what was by then the See of Glasgow. He restored rights and possessions that it had lost over time. The See thrived during the following centuries and, given its growing status in land, wealth and power, it also became involved in many aspects of the entire country's affairs.

The medieval Bishop's Palace and castle to the left and the cathedral from the south-west.

The actual size of the cathedral revealed from the Necropolis.

In the early fourteenth century the Bishop of Glasgow, Robert Wishart (or Wischard), openly and actively supported King Robert the Bruce in the war to maintain Scottish independence. He had already absolved the Bruce for killing the Red Comyn in 1306 and in the war with King Edward I Wishart did whatever he could to help King Robert. This included using wood provided for the construction of the cathedral spire to build catapults for his king. Wishart was finally caught by the English and imprisoned until the overwhelming Scottish victory at Bannockburn in 1314.

The see became an archbishopric in 1492 but in 1560 the authority of the Catholic Church ended in Scotland with the Reformation. Archbishop Beaton fled to France with the cathedral's treasures, and much of the land accruing to the cathedral was eventually spirited away by opportunists. There followed periods of Episcopalian and Presbyterian rule which finally ended in 1690 with the establishment of the Presbyterian Church of Scotland.

Glasgow's cathedral was saved when others had been destroyed in the Reformation but it had been damaged and later fell into disrepair. It survived because it became useful again. Its interior was eventually divided into three churches to meet the needs of new parishes.

The cathedral is the oldest structure in the city and the oldest cathedral on mainland Scotland. No remains of the earliest buildings have been found on the cathedral site, but this is not unexpected as Celtic community buildings would have been constructed with wattle, wood and daub. Such materials usually decompose. The first known mortared stone building was dedicated in 1136 but it was burned down in 1197. The cathedral was rebuilt and developed in various

St Mungo's tomb in the crypt.

phases. Over the years, the east end of the cathedral was extended down the slope towards the Molendinar burn so that St Mungo's tomb could be incorporated into the building to safeguard and honour it. This extension has been noted as 'one of the greatest architectural treasures of the medieval period in Scotland'.

By around 1330 the cathedral finally looked much like the present building. Inevitably, over time, such structures still deteriorate and require restoration. By the early Victorian era it was in a sad condition. Luckily, it was saved when its architecture and history were 'rediscovered'. The cathedral was restored but unfortunately two ancient towers to the west of the building were demolished by enthusiastic Victorians who misjudged their provenance.

Glasgow cathedral is generally considered to be Scotland's greatest and best-preserved church of the Gothic period. It is now in the care of Historic Environment Scotland.

13. CHURCH ON THE HILL/LANGSIDE HILL CHURCH OF SCOTLAND
16 Algie St, Langside, G41 3DJ

Langside Hill Free Church opened in 1896. It was designed by Alexander Skirving, a former assistant to Alexander 'Greek' Thomson. Thomson's influence can be seen in the classical Graeco-Roman style which he used in his Caledonia Road church. The pediment above the colonnade of Langside Hill church was intended to contain a depiction of John Knox arguing with Queen Mary, echoing the historical association with the area, but this did not materialise. The site for

The Church on the Hill and the Battle Monument.

the church is to the west of the Battle Monument – also designed by Skirving – erected in 1887–88.

The two structures sit atop the hill near to where, on 13 May, 1568, the Protestant Regent Moray arrayed his army of around 2,000 men, many from nearby Glasgow, to confront the Catholic Mary, Queen of Scots' army of around 6,000. Confident that her numbers would easily defeat Moray, Mary enjoined battle only to be completely defeated. She fled the field and Scotland eventually to be imprisoned for the rest of her life in Elizabeth I's England until her execution.

The Langside Hill church eventually united with the Church of Scotland in 1929. Fifty years later, the congregation joined the nearby Battlefield East Church, and sold their own premises. The building lay unused for a lengthy period of time and was badly vandalised. Fortunately, it was rescued for posterity when it was converted into a restaurant – the Church on the Hill.

14. COMMITTEE ROOM NO. 9/JOHN STREET CHURCH OF SCOTLAND
18 John St, Merchant City

A church was opened on this site in 1798 for a breakaway group from the first Relief congregation in Glasgow, at Dovehill near the Gallowgate. It was known as the John Street Relief Church. The original John Street building was replaced in 1859 by the magnificent structure here today. However, it eventually closed in 1972 as a Church of Scotland.

One of Glasgow's old city centre churches.

The building was sold to the what was then Glasgow Corporation and was used as a night shelter for homeless men. When the Kirkhaven project at the Trinity Duke St Church building in Duke St (now Glasgow Building Preservation Trust) was opened and took over this work, the John Street building was sold. Subsequently, the interior of the building was converted to commercial use in 1987–88. It has since been used as a bar and for functions under a variety of names including John Street Jam and the Rat & Parrot. Currently it is Committee Room No. 9, probably reflecting the very close proximity of its one-time owner – Glasgow City Chambers.

15. COTTIERS/DOWANHILL CHURCH OF SCOTLAND
93–95 Hyndland St, Dowanhill, G11 5PU

The story of the origin of Downfield Church was probably repeated again and again in villages and towns across Scotland at a time when several denominations were emerging in competition with the Established Church.

Dowanhill – the descendant of Partick's first church.

Prior to 1823 there was no church in Partick village. Preachers of various denominations would visit to deliver sermons but there was no dedicated building. The Church of Scotland Parish Church for Partick was situated in Govan. To reach it, the villagers had to cross the Clyde – albeit far shallower at that time. There were stepping stones across the river but people occasionally fell in, so there was also a ferry.

In 1823 some interested parties sounded out the villagers' view of having a church built in Partick. It was agreeable to many but of which denomination it should be became a major issue. As a result, both the Relief and United Secession decided to build churches. They both started building late in 1823, and the United Secession completed first in May 1824. It was known as the Associate Congregation of Partick.

A superb new replacement church was opened in 1866 and still dominates the view to the north along Hyndland Street. Its congregation terminated in 1984 as Dowanhill Church of Scotland and then entered into the religious history of nearby Partick Trinity. By this time, Dowanhill had required major repair and restoration works. Fortunately, this was undertaken over an extended period by the Four Acres Charitable Trust which acquired it in 1984. The building has taken on a new identity as Cottiers pub, restaurant and theatre, and named after Daniel Cottier who created the internationally important stained glass that remains in the church.

16. Deeper Life Bible Church
85 Killin St, Shettleston, G32 9AH

Shettleston is the location of a very old settlement, with its earliest potential reference being in a Papal Bull of 1179 sent to the Bishop of Glasgow. This referred to the 'villam filie Sedin' – the residence of Sedin's son or daughter. The district fell within the original Barony Parish which, by the mid-eighteenth century, could not meet the needs of a growing congregation living at a considerable distance from the Barony church. Eventually the local people decided to build a church for themselves which opened in 1752 under the authority of the Barony. In 1847 it became Shettleston Parish Church of Scotland.

Over time the church required replacement, partly due to coal being illegally mined beneath it and causing subsidence. However, this was not achieved until 1902 after a court action known as the Shettleston Church Case. Revd John White initiated the process which succeeded in compelling the heritors of the parish (generally, property owners) to pay their dues towards building it. The new church was built in Killin Street. The old church was demolished in 1909 but the walled cemetery still survives. The money raised also paid for the building of St Margaret's, Tollcross and St Michael's, Carntyne.

With the 1929 union of UF and Established Churches Shettleston was obliged to alter its name to Shettleston Old Parish Church. It was now located in close proximity to other churches of the same denomination. In later years, with a diminishing congregation and the need for very costly repairs, this combination led to Shettleston's closure in 2015 and its sale. The current occupiers of the buildings are the Deeper Life Bible Church and the Romanian Orthodox Church in Scotland.

Above: Deeper Life Bible Church and Hall.

Below: Interior while still Shettleston Old at Christmas.

17. DENNISTOUN NEW PARISH CHURCH OF SCOTLAND & ST KENTIGERN'S CHAPEL

9 Armadale St, Dennistoun, G31 2UU

Until 2007 Dennistoun New was Dennistoun Central. The change took place when the congregation of its neighbouring Dennistoun Blackfriars united with it. The structure, which tends to be considered as a 'traditional' Victorian style

Dennistoun New Parish Church.

St Kentigern's Scottish
Episcopal Church.

of architecture, was built in 1874 as a Free Church. In 2003 its minister, Adah Younger, was the first woman to become Moderator of Glasgow Presbytery. Unusually, since 1983, the church has hosted St Kentigern's Scottish Episcopal congregation at a small chapel in the north aisle. This was a composite of two churches which had closed – Holy Trinity, Riddrie and St Barnabus, Craigpark.

18. FREE CHURCH COLLEGE & THE PARK CHURCH
Lynedoch Crescent & Street, Woodlands, G3 6AA

The triple towers of the old Free Church College (1856–57) and the neighbouring single tower of what was the Park Church of Scotland (1858) dominate the surrounding landscape of their setting on their hilltop in east Woodlands. Seen from the west at Garnethill.

This nineteenth-century print of the same buildings is drawn from Somerset Place at Sauchiehall Street, looking north.

19. GARNETHILL SYNAGOGUE
129 Hill St, Garnethill, G3 6UB

There does not seem to be any evidence of Jewish people practising their religion in Scotland until 1691 – a David Brown, living in Edinburgh. From the late eighteenth century there was an influx of Jewish refugees from Europe resulting from the French Revolution and the subsequent Napoleonic Wars. Most of these landed on the east coast of the country and it took time for individuals to make their way across to Glasgow. The first known record of a Jewish resident in Glasgow was in 1812. This was Isaac Cohen, a hatter.

Numbers increased slowly and it was not until 1823 that there were enough to form a small congregation. In that year, the first noted location for worship in Glasgow was in two rooms of a family's home within a tenement flat, at No. 43 High Street. By 1831 it was estimated that there were still only forty-seven individuals in the city, only twenty-eight of whom were over twenty years old. The congregation continued to grow and moved on from the High Street to a number of subsequent locations.

In 1858, a synagogue was relocated to No. 240 George Street which had accommodation for 260. By 1870 there were still only two synagogues in Scotland – one in Glasgow and another in Edinburgh. The Glasgow synagogue in George Street was increasingly unable to accommodate its congregation and it

Garnethill Synagogue sits atop the highest hill in the city centre which can present quite a challenging climb from Sauchiehall Street.

was this that finally led to the building of the Garnethill synagogue. This opened in 1879 and continues to provide its services to its community.

20. GLASGOW ASSOCIATION FOR MENTAL HEALTH/ST ANDREW'S BY THE GREEN
33 Turnbull St, G1 5PR

The Episcopal Meeting House of St Andrew's was built in 1750 on Willow Acre, an area of land beside the Molendinar Burn and Glasgow Green. It was erected in a remarkably short time after the 1745 Jacobite Rebellion, when there was still considerable government and local hostility towards the Scottish Episcopal Church for its apparent support of the Stuart usurper Bonnie Prince Charlie. The fact that St Andrew's was not a Scottish Episcopal Church made no difference. When one of the builders of the 'English Chapel' refused to stop working on it he was excommunicated from his own church for the offence.

Feelings ran so high that even the speed with which the chapel was built was the subject of gossip. Nearby St Andrew's Parish Church of Scotland was still under construction after eleven years (and not completed until 1756), while the chapel was raised in little more than a single year. Such speed could only be the result of diabolic intervention! Several accounts describe the role of 'Nickey Ben' (the Devil). One old woman swore she had seen him early one morning doing the work of ten men. On being greeted by a 'Fine Mornin', Mem' she retorted, 'Ye Black Deevil, in the name of God, come awa' frae that Whore of Babylon.'

St Andrew's closed in 1974 and in 1988 it was converted into offices. It is now reckoned to be the oldest existing Episcopal church building in Scotland and currently accommodates Glasgow Association for Mental Health.

His ears being assaulted by the use of the 'Divine Name' Lucifer vanished in 'Fire and Brimstone' (Gordon, 1872).

The chapel met the needs of the local English aristocracy, gentry and merchants, as well as the military from the Gallowgate Barracks in later years. It is also said that James Wolfe, hero of the Canadian wars, attended while he lived at Camlachie.

21. GLASGOW BUILDING PRESERVATION TRUST/TRINITY DUKE STREET CHURCH OF SCOTLAND

176 Duke St, Dennistoun, G4 0UW

The East End's very own Greek temple is situated in Duke Street. The street was opened in 1794 and named for the Duke of Montrose who had a residence there. At one time, it was agreed as being the longest street in the UK but it may or may not have the same accolade these days.

This church is one of the few significant buildings surviving in Duke Street. A major attribute of the church is what has been described as 'one of the finest ornate plaster ceilings in Glasgow'. The church was built in 1857–58 as Sydney Street United Presbyterian Church, originating from the East Campbell Street First UP Church. A number of other congregations joined over the years and it

The buildings were restored between 2000–03 and are now A listed. The old church has been converted to provide multi-level office space which can be readily removed should the building ever need to revert to its original purpose.

eventually became Trinity Duke Street Church of Scotland in 1949. In its turn, the congregation left to join Rutherford Church in 1975 to form Dennistoun Central Church of Scotland which continues as Dennistoun New.

The Duke Street buildings were acquired by the Church's Board of Social Responsibility and converted for use as a night shelter for homeless men, to be known as Kirkhaven. The project moved to a tenement property in Dalmarnock in 1996 after the buildings were damaged by fire and were subsequently acquired by the Glasgow Building Preservation Trust. The Trust is a charity whose purpose is 'to rescue, repair, restore and rehabilitate historic buildings at risk across the city'.

22. GLASGOW CITY FREE CHURCH
265 St Vincent St, City Centre, G2 7LQ

Four churches were built by Alexander 'Greek' Thomson in Glasgow. His fourth was Queens Park UP (1868–1943) which was destroyed in the bombing of Glasgow in the Second World War. His third was Chalmers Memorial Free in the Gorbals which was used by the congregation from its opening in 1859 until the turn of the century when the congregation moved to the new Cunninghame Memorial Church. The Thomson church was then used by a number of commercial enterprises until it burnt down in 1971.

His first church, Caledonia Road UP, opened in 1857 and also experienced a major fire, but much was salvaged. It remains as a significant landmark in the Gorbals. His second is the Glasgow City Free Church which was initially designated as the St Vincent Street UP Church. It is the only one to have survived intact and still in use as it was intended. The building is certainly a very dramatic

The A listed building is owned by Glasgow City Council and the fortunate occupant has been there since 1971.

structure with the exterior exhibiting a comprehensive range of architectural forms from ancient Greece, Egypt and possibly even India.

Thomson was himself a member of the UP Church for which he mostly built. A celebrated American architectural historian, Henry-Russell Hitchcock, described Thomson as one of the two 'greatest architects of the Western world', the other being Charles Rennie Mackintosh.

23. GLASGOW EVANGELICAL CHURCH
14–20 Cathedral Square, Townhead, G4 0XA

This highly ornate, Italianate-style church dominates the south-eastern corner of Cathedral Square and was A listed in 1970. It was built in 1878–80 to a design by John Honeyman for descendants of the old Havannah Anti-Burgher Church in Duke Street. As a United Presbyterian congregation, it moved from its original premises when its land was sold to the North British Railway. When it relocated, it took the Cathedral Square name and later became part of the Church of Scotland.

By 1941 the congregation had decided to quit the building as the result of declining numbers and join the Regent Place Church in Dennistoun. On the night of the very last service, the neighbouring Barony North Church of Scotland across

The above photograph was taken in 1999 and this view to the front of the building is now obscured by trees.

the Square suffered a disastrous fire. Luckily, a move could be made immediately by its congregation to the vacated building, while retaining its own name. A new home had been found for the next thirty-eight years, finally dissolving as a congregation in 1979.

Through the years its condition had gradually deteriorated and it faced a rather uncertain future until it was rescued by the Glasgow Evangelical Church. The building was acquired for a nominal sum, and as the result of its efforts from the beginning of the 1980s the new congregation raised a considerable amount to undertake repairs. Some members even learned the skills of creating stained-glass windows and installed some of their own creations in the church.

It seems appropriate that the church is overlooked by the nearby John Knox statue atop the Glasgow Necropolis, while the equestrian statue of William III stands in the gardens to the front. Both have been a significant influence for the church and its congregation's beliefs.

24. GLASGOW HINDU MANDIR & CULTURAL CENTRE
1 La Belle Place, Finnieston, G3 7LH

The original title of the Queen's Rooms is suggestive of a Jane Austen novel and an early nineteenth-century ballroom. Presumably taking its name from the reigning monarch of the time, Queen Victoria, it was built in 1857 to a design by Charles Wilson. The building is enhanced by a wealth of sculpture by John Mossman on the north and east façades which has survived largely intact. The Mossman family were prolific Glasgow sculptors and their work can still be found throughout the city.

Above left and above right: Glasgow Hindu Mandir and a detail of the shrine room.

The building's attraction was further enhanced by its close proximity to the new Kelvingrove Park. Wilson himself had provided the initial plan for the park to the town council in 1851.

The owner's intention was to attract the local residents from what was a new and well-to-do suburb of Glasgow. The main entertainment to be provided would seem to have been concerts. The appeal of the Rooms was successful and it continued in business until 1912. The building was later acquired by the First Church of Christ Scientist. Williamson et al. (1990) indicates that the original interior was stripped while being converted for the church in 1948. At present No. 1 La Belle Place is home to the Glasgow Hindu Mandir, a mandir being a Hindu temple, with the principal space being used for that purpose. The mandir also provides a wide range of activities and support to its community.

25. GLASGOW REFORMED PRESBYTERIAN CHURCH OF SCOTLAND
10 Muirpark St, Partick, G11 5NP

It is reckoned that the population of Partick rose from around 2,000 inhabitants in 1843 to over 35,000 by 1876. This remarkable increase was the result of immigration into the whole of the Glasgow area due to the advance of the Industrial Revolution and its need for workers. A significant portion of the new inhabitants in Partick were Gaelic speakers from the Highlands and the West of Scotland.

From around 1864, Anderson Free Church made efforts in Partick to engage with the Gaelic speakers with the result that a congregation was sanctioned by the Free Church in 1887. Temporary accommodation was found – a reused iron building – until the church hall was built in Gardner Street. This was named the Partick Free Gaelic Church. It was not until 1905 (dates vary) that the church building itself was completed.

Through the years, the congregation engaged in the major reunions of the various denominations until it became Partick Gardner Street Church of Scotland

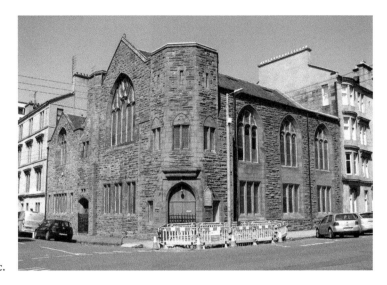

The church closed in *c.* 2011 and was subsequently acquired by its present resident. However, St Columba Gaelic Church of Scotland in Glasgow's city centre continues to provide services in Gaelic.

in 1929. Not all of the congregation followed this course of action and some chose to worship elsewhere.

There is still a shop in Partick which sells Gaelic books and resources, which suggests there remains a Gaelic community – or at least a community of the interested – in the district.

26. GLASGOW ROYAL INFIRMARY CHAPEL, TOWNHEAD
84 Castle St, G4 0SF

Shown right is one of the stained-glass windows in the chapel of Glasgow Royal Infirmary, depicting the care of the sick. The inscriptions read:

'Inasmuch as ye have done it unto the least of these ye have done it unto me'

'This window erected by past and present nurses of the Royal Infirmary 1912'

Glasgow Royal Infirmary dates back to 1794, with buildings continually being updated and more being added to the extensive complex over the centuries. Most hospitals in Glasgow provide a quiet space for patients, visitors and staff to rest and contemplate. In the Centre Block of the older part of the Royal is a small chapel for this purpose. It is for any person who wishes to use it and is available twenty-four hours a day. There is also access to a chaplaincy service.

27. GLASGOW'S GURDWARAS: CENTRAL GURDWARA SINGH SAHBA
138 Berkeley St, Finnieston, G3 7HY

North of the Clyde is the Central Gurdwara which opened in 2016, adding beautifully to Glasgow's skyline. It originated from a group of twenty Sikhs who established a Trust in 1981 for the benefit of an expanding Sikh community. It is not simply a place for worship, but also a multi-functional resource.

28. GLASGOW GURDWARA GURU GRANTH SAHIB SIKH SABHA
35 Albert Drive, Pollokshields, G41 2PE

South of the Clyde is the Glasgow Gurdwara which opened in April 2013. Prior to this, a large Victorian building in Nithsdale Road was used for the purpose for over fifty years and was recorded as the first dedicated location for a Sikh gurdwara in Scotland. It was established in the 1960s for both Sikhs and non-Sikhs and became a focus for a wide variety of beneficial community activities.

29. GOVAN & LINTHOUSE PARISH CHURCH OF SCOTLAND
796 Govan Rd, Govan, G51 2YL

Its current designation is the result of its union with two other local churches in 2008 – Linthouse St Kenneth's in Skipness Drive and nearby Govan Old Parish

This recently restored church started as St Mary's Govan Free Church congregation in 1872, with the church opening the following year.

The image above of *c.* 1910 shows the precinct in front of the church was popular for gatherings. The tenements to the left have now gone, as has the tower and spire of the church, but most of the buildings on the right have survived.

Church which is now in the care of the Govan Heritage Trust. The Linthouse building is currently in use by the Salvation Army while repairs are made to its own premises.

30. GOVANHILL WORKSPACE/NEW BRIDGEGATE CHURCH OF SCOTLAND
69 Dixon Rd, Govanhill, G42 8AT

The original Bridgegate Free Church was built in 1860 in Glasgow's Bridgegate (or Briggait). Medieval Glasgow was never a walled town, but it still had gates, or gaits, on major roads which served to restrict access to the town when necessary. At the Briggait, traffic crossing into Glasgow over its only bridge on the Clyde could be controlled.

The building was sold in 1915 and demolished to facilitate the ongoing construction of the city's railways. A replacement was built in Govanhill from 1921 and was named the New Bridgegate. A souvenir of the old building was incorporated into the new structure. The old church is said to have been the last to have an external pulpit from which passers-by could be sermonised, lectured or challenged. This could lead to large crowds gathering which blocked the street and sometimes rioted. Eventually, the city fathers banned the practice. When the old church was being taken down, the stone bookrest of the external pulpit was saved and built into the new church's exterior.

The present church was closed in 1991. It was acquired by Govanhill Housing Association in 1994 which converted it into multi-functional areas and renamed it as Govanhill Workspace.

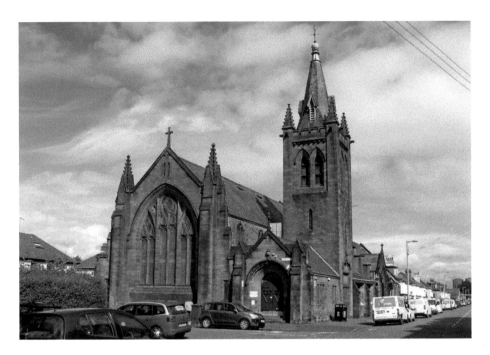

Above: Govanhill Workplace, previously New Bridgegate Church.

Right: The exterior pulpit of the original church in Bridgegate.

31. GOVAN OLD CHURCH OF SCOTLAND, GOVAN/THE GOVAN STONES
866 Govan Rd, Govan, G51 7UU

Govan and Glasgow both seem to have developed Christian settlements by the sixth century and lived a similar existence for a considerable period of time. However, given the remarkable archaeological relics found in Govan Old's graveyard, there was probably a Viking settlement in Govan for a time.

While Glasgow had its St Mungo, Govan had his contemporary in St Constantine who had once been King of Cornwall until he gave up his throne to preach Christianity. He travelled north and eventually arrived at Govan where a monastery was founded. When Constantine died during his further travels, he was brought back to Govan. A current legend is that he was buried in the sarcophagus discovered in the Govan churchyard.

With the relentless growth of Glasgow Cathedral's Barony domain Govan was eventually absorbed into it in the twelfth century when it was given to the cathedral by King David I. The Barony, as property, effectively ended with the Reformation and the lands subsequently acquired by a number of lay people.

In later years Govan does not seem to have engaged with the Industrial Revolution as fully or as quickly as Glasgow. In the early nineteenth century it was still being described as rural in appearance. Inevitably, the times caught up with Govan and that rural aspect was rapidly destroyed. It gained burgh status in 1862 and in 1912 it was incorporated into municipal Glasgow.

The old building is now in the care of the Govan Heritage Trust and is used by the 'Govan Stones' project, which safeguards and displays Govan's relics. However, after around 1,400 years, worship still takes place in the old church on weekdays. The Russian Orthodox Church also uses the building.

The present church opened in 1888. Govan Old's congregation was one of the three that recently united to form Govan & Linthouse Parish Church of Scotland in 2008.

32. GREEK ORTHODOX CATHEDRAL OF ST LUKE THE EVANGELIST SCOTLAND

27 Dundonald Rd, Dowanhill, G12 9LL

Glasgow-born architect James Sellars designed many well-known buildings in the city, including Fraser's store in Buchanan Street, the Couper Institute and St Andrew's Halls (now the Mitchell Theatre). He also designed the Belhaven UP Church of 1874–75 which he himself attended. It later united with the Church of Scotland and eventually terminated in 1960 when the congregation joined the Westbourne Church, now Struthers Memorial Pentecostal Church.

The original Bellhaven Church, now a cathedral.

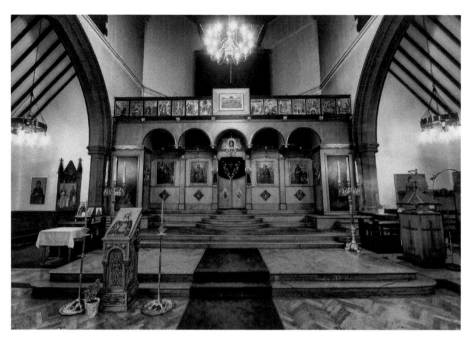

The templon of the Greek Orthodox Cathedral of St Luke the Evangelist Scotland.

A Greek community had been established in Scotland by 1944 which was able to use a number of Scottish churches for worship until 1953 when they moved to their own building in Grafton St. This had been bought for the community by well-known Glasgow restaurateur Reo Stakis. 10 years later he also helped facilitate the purchase of the vacant Belhaven Church which was to become St Luke's. In 1970 the church was elevated to the status of Cathedral by Pope and Patriarch of Alexandria, Nicholas VI when he visited Scotland to attend the General Assembly of the Church of Scotland.

33. KELVINBRIDGE PARISH CHURCH OF SCOTLAND
62 Belmont St, North Kelvinside, G20 6JR

In 2013 the congregation of the Lansdowne church (now Webster's Theatre) in Great Western Road joined that of Kelvin Stevenson Memorial to form the present congregation of Kelvinbridge Church. The building was opened in 1902 as the Nathaniel Stevenson Memorial Free Church, named for his father by its benefactor James Stevenson, and designed by the latter's nephew. The church is a mix of *c.* fourteenth-century English and *c.* fifteenth-century Scottish Gothic design according to Williamson et al. (1990).

The church is situated on a quite dramatic spot. The River Kelvin runs through a valley immediately to the south of the building which is perched above the precipitous fall. The breathtaking drop is even more accentuated by the height of the building, particularly the tower at the north-west surmounted by a crown steeple.

It is a pity that the sculptures beneath the parapet of the steeple are less visible – they are comprised of a variety of subjects which include squirrels and a monkey – binoculars are recommended.

34. KELVINGROVE CHURCH OF SCOTLAND
49 Derby St, Kelvingrove, G3 7TY

The Finnieston Free Church congregation was an offshoot of Free St Matthew's and opened its first building in 1857 at the corner of Finnieston Street and Houldsworth Street. Its second home was built in Derby Street from 1876–78 and remained as Finnieston Free Church. This elegant structure was constructed to a 'Greek Revival' design by James Seller.

On 13 March 1941 a landmine exploded nearby at the bridge over the River Kelvin. The church suffered significant blast damage and was closed for around eighteen months for repairs, but it survived and has enhanced the landscape ever since. After several unions and reunions, it finally closed in 1979 as Kelvingrove Church of Scotland and joined the nearby Anderson church which became Anderson Kelvingrove, now part of St Andrew's West Church of Scotland.

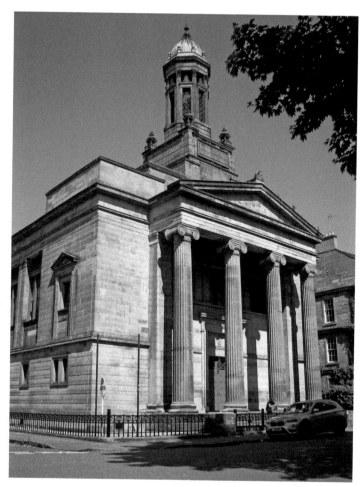

The church was sold to Ca-Va Recording Studios, which was very well known in the music industry. Eventually, this A listed property was converted into flats around 2009 for some very fortunate people.

35. KNIGHTSWOOD ST MARGARET'S PARISH CHURCH OF SCOTLAND
2000 Great Western Rd, Knightswood, G13 2HA

In 1925 a new congregation was formed in the recently developed Glasgow suburb of Knightswood, using a hall until it could build a church. The result was this beautiful Scottish fortified tower house of a building of 1929–32. Its medieval appearance seems entirely appropriate for its patron saint, the eleventh-century St Margaret, Queen of Scotland.

As Margaret of Wessex, an English princess, she married King Malcolm III of Scotland (1070–93) after her family had fled England following the invasion by William the Conqueror in 1066. Margaret was very religious and highly supportive of the Roman Catholic Church, as eventually was her son King David I. Inevitably this support was detrimental to the Celtic practices which had developed in Scotland. Margaret died in 1093, just three days after her husband, and was buried in Dunfermline Abbey. She was canonised in 1250.

Several other churches have also taken the name of St Margaret in Glasgow, including St Margaret's Polmadie and St Margaret's Episcopal Church.

36. KURDISH COMMUNITY & EDUCATION CENTRE/ AL TAWHEED MOSQUE

179 Braidfauld Gardens, Tollcross, G32 8PG

It was not until 1901 that the Church of Scotland finally built its first church in Tollcross – St Margaret's Tollcross. Before then, parishioners were still obliged to attend the old church at Shettleston which had become structurally dangerous. When the Revd John White of Shettleston won a celebrated legal case against the heritors of his parish, forcing them to meet their financial obligations, the resulting funds paid for St Margaret's Tollcross as well as a new Shettleston Church, currently the Deeper Life Bible Church.

St Margaret's was one of the first churches to draw my attention to the need to replace pews with chairs. As well as meeting new requirements to facilitate access by disabled parishioners it created space for other activities. Also, it had not gone unnoticed that some present-day worshippers were somewhat 'larger' than their forefathers and could find squeezing into a pew problematic.

St Margaret's was eventually joined by the nearby Tollcross Park congregation in 1994 to become St Margaret's Tollcross Park, but due to diminishing numbers, it also had to close. When the United Free Church and

Sadly, the trees which enhanced this old church were recently removed.

the Church of Scotland unified in 1929 there were then three Churches of Scotland in Tollcross, but with the closure of St Margaret's there remains only one – the Causeway Church. Happily, St Margaret's did not suffer the same fate of some others and the lovely Arts & Crafts building was saved when it was purchased in 2019 to become the home of the Al-Tawheed Mosque & Kurdish Community & Education Centre.

37. LANGSIDE HEBREW CONGREGATION SYNAGOGUE
125 Niddrie Rd, Queen's Park, G42 8QA

As the Jewish population of the south side of the city grew significantly there was increasingly less enthusiasm to make their way across the river then be faced with the steep climb to the summit of Garnethill to attend the synagogue there. One consequence of this was the foundation of Langside Synagogue in 1915. It was situated in what was then Cromwell Road which became Langside Road in the 1930s.

The congregation had a new home built in Niddrie Road in 1926–27. This was designed by Jeffrey, Waddell & Young with a pleasant Romanesque façade to the east. However, the synagogue was closed in 2014 for the usual reason of declining numbers attending.

In 2020 the synagogue was C-listed recognising its architectural importance.

In 2019 a local group designating themselves as the 'Irn-Ju' (presumably a take on the popular Scottish soft drink Irn Bru) started a campaign to save the synagogue from demolition or conversion into housing. They were seeking to have it restored to its original use and as a community resource.

38. MALMAISON GLASGOW/ST JUDE'S FREE PRESBYTERIAN CHURCH
278 West George St, City Centre, G2 4LL

The Malmaison building with its notably massive entrance dates from 1838 and was originally a Scottish Episcopal Church named St Jude's. Above the entrance in Greek lettering is an inscription which states 'Christ is the Head of the Church' – although there is said to be an error in the script. The church was ordered to be built by Bishop Russell for a part of the congregation of St Mary's Chapel in Renfield Street that wished to be led by an alternative priest.

The congregation did not succeed as well as it had hoped and its locale was becoming less agreeable. In 1844 it withdrew from the Scottish Church and in 1862 some of the more well-to-do members left to form a new chapel in the west end – St Silas Episcopal Church. By 1875 some of the remaining members of St Jude's had returned to St Mary's. In later years those who were left experienced severe financial difficulties and lost the building. Some remnants of the congregation then moved to St Barnabus in the east end which is now part of St Kentigern's in Dennistoun New Church of Scotland.

The new owners of the building eventually rented it to a Free Presbyterian congregation in 1893 which took the St Jude name. That congregation then bought it in 1909. It moved in 1975 after purchasing what is now St Jude's Free Presbyterian Church in Woodlands Road. The old building was converted into office space known as St Jude's House until Malmaison Glasgow took it over in 1994.

39. OUR LADY OF GOOD COUNSEL ROMAN CATHOLIC CHURCH
60 Craigpark, Dennistoun, G31 2NN

The origins of the 'Good Counsel' part of this church's name seems uncertain – one suggestion is that in the fifteenth century two young men, devotees of Mary, were advised by her to leave Albania as the Turks were invading. In doing so their lives were presumably saved.

Our Lady of Good Counsel is quite a dramatic building of 1965 by Jack Coia, described by his biographer as having a 'soaring, tent-like copper roof above the sanctuary' and designed to create more subdued light for the interior as opposed to the bright light sought by many other churches.

Jack Coia (1898–1981) was a very well-known Glasgow architect who undertook the design of a large number of churches and other buildings, particularly in Glasgow. His father was an immigrant from the Filignano district of Italy and Jack was born in Wolverhampton. While he was still young his family moved to Glasgow where his father opened one of the first Italian cafés in the city in Parkhead. Jack attended the local school at St Michael's Primary.

He eventually became a member of the architectural partnership of Gillespie, Kidd & Coia. Some of his other Glasgow churches include nearby St Anne's RC in Dennistoun, St Paul's RC in Shettleston and St Columba of Iona RC in Maryhill.

40. PARTICK FREE CHURCH OF SCOTLAND
29 Crow Rd, Partick, G11 7RT

Over a period of ten years (the Ten Years Conflict) a very large number of the Church of Scotland membership became increasingly opposed to what they considered to be interference by the Government in the spiritual independence of the Church. At the General Assembly in Edinburgh of May 1843 this culminated in the withdrawal of around one third of those attending and their immediate inauguration of the Free Church of Scotland. This event has been recorded in

Partick Free, which
remained in the
Free Church at the
Disruption.

history as the Disruption. It created great hardship for many, both for those leaving the Established Church and for those remaining. By 1929 many had eventually returned to the Church of Scotland, but not all. Partick Free was built in 1910.

41. PARTICK FREE CHURCH OF SCOTLAND (CONTINUING)
2–4 Thornwood Terrace, Broomhill, G11 7QZ

In 2000 the Free Church divided on the basis of who maintained 'continuity with the Church of 1843, the system of doctrine and the form of worship adopted by the Church of Scotland at the Reformation'. Some members of the Partick Free

When the United Free congregation was terminated in 2018 for lack of numbers, Partick Free (Continuing) purchased the Broomhill buildings.

Church congregation felt they could no longer remain and left to form the Partick Free Church of Scotland (Continuing). Partick United Free Church in Broomhill allowed the new congregation to share its church for its own services.

42. PARTICK TRINITY CHURCH OF SCOTLAND
20 Lawrence St, Dowanhill, G11 5HG

Partick Trinity had a close association with the congregation of nearby Dowanhill Church for a very long time, originating as it did from missionary work which Dowanhill had helped undertake. When sufficient numbers had been achieved for the creation of the new congregation it purchased Dowanhill's old church at the bottom of Byres Road in 1866 and took the name Partick East UP. The congregation remained there for thirty-three years until it moved to their new home in Lawrence Street, taking their name with them.

In 1984 when the congregation of Dowanhill was terminated the remnant was taken in by Partick East to form Partick East & Dowanhill Church of Scotland. Later, in 1994, it also took in the remaining congregation of the Old Partick Parish Church in Church Street. With that last union, the church changed to its present name with a trinity of congregations forming its history. This adoption of 'Trinity' in a name seems to be a fairly common practice in similar circumstances.

Partick Trinity was built in 1899 to a Scots Late Gothic design in what is described as red rock-faced rubble – a material frequently used in the city – and opened in 1899.

This view of Pollokshields West is only
available at certain times of the year,
otherwise it can become too well screened
by trees to fully appreciate it.

43. POLLOKSHIELDS WEST CHURCH OF SCOTLAND
620 Shields Rd, Pollokshields, G41 2RD

A Free Church congregation started in 1875 in an iron building, as many others did
before them, while awaiting the construction of their stone edifice. Pollokshields
West was built in 1875–79. Its role as a church ended in 1963 when it joined
nearby Trinity Pollokshields, the latter becoming Pollokshields Glencairn. The
building is currently occupied by a number of businesses including a children's
nursery and a nursing home.

It was designed by W. G. Rowan and is reminiscent of 'Greek' Thomson's
huge scale of building. Williamson et al. (1990) suggest that the corner tower is
modelled on St George's Tron. It can be interesting to compare the different works
of an architect and in this instance one very much in contrast to Pollokshield's
West is Rowan's lovely Arts & Crafts, English-style 'village' church of the Kurdish
Community/Al Tawheed Mosque.

44. QUEEN'S CROSS
870 Garscube Rd, Maryhill, G20 7EL

In 1896 St Matthew Free Church commissioned a new church and hall for their
Springbank mission from architects Honeyman & Keppie. The task fell to a
new trainee – with the most sublime good luck – as Charles Rennie Macintosh
(1868–1928) produced his one and only entire church. Situated at the junction of
Garscube Road and Maryhill Road, it is visited by Macintosh aficionados from
around the world. Both interior and exterior designs have survived almost intact
and are instantly recognised as the Macintosh style of Art Nouveau.

Queen's Cross was opened in 1899 and eventually became a Church of Scotland in 1929.

It was joined by the congregation of St Cuthbert's in 1954 to become St Cuthbert's & Queen's Cross but closed in 1976 on uniting with Ruchill. The usual fate of many such churches at the time was demolition or conversion to housing or commercial premises. However, the A listed building's future was safeguarded when it was acquired by the Charles Rennie Macintosh Society. It is now simply known by its original name of Queen's Cross.

There are other examples of Macintosh's work distributed throughout the city, one nearby being the church hall of Ruchill Kelvinside Church of Scotland, also in Maryhill.

45. QUEEN'S PARK SYNAGOGUE
1 Falloch Rd, Battlefield, G42 9QX

The entrance to a surprisingly pink Queen's Park Synagogue.

Rear view of the synagogue.

This B listed synagogue was opened in 1926, recorded as the year 5686 in the Jewish calendar on an inscription above the main entrance. It is unexpectedly large and impressive compared to others in the city. The congregation was founded in 1906 and used a variety of sites, including a 'tin schul' from 1917, until the building of Queen's Park.

The synagogue closed on 16 September 2002 after a Yom Kippur service, and merged with the Netherlee & Clarkston Hebrew Congregation to form the Netherlee, Clarkston & Queen's Park Hebrew Congregation which closed in 2012. The Queen's Park building was converted into flats in 2008.

46. RE-HOPE – SOUTHSIDE
14 Regwood St, Shawlands, G41 3JG

To the rear of this church is a building which very much appears to be another one. In fact, it is the original hall of 1909 which was used by South Shawlands until its actual church was built to the east and opened in 1913. The congregation occupied South Shawlands until 2017, at which time it united with Shawlands to form Shawlands Trinity. The building was subsequently sold to RE-HOPE.

47. RE-HOPE – West End
37 Stewartville St, Partick, G11 5PL

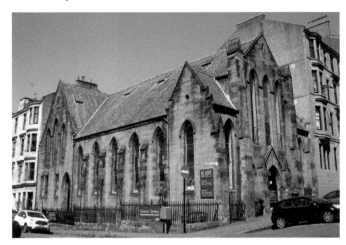

As Partick Congregational building this red-sandstone church was built in 1910. The façade is reputed to have been modelled on the east front of Dunblane Cathedral. It is currently occupied by RE-HOPE.

48. Romanian Orthodox Church in Scotland –
Glasgow Parish

111 Killin St, Shettleston, G32 9AH

In 2009, the congregation of Shettleston Old Parish Church let its church hall to the Romanian Orthodox Church. In doing so it facilitated the first Romanian Orthodox place of worship in Scotland, with its inauguration ceremony held on 18 January, 2009. Its interior is shown below.

When the Shettleston Old congregation finally had to quit its own home in 2015 to join to what is now the Causeway Church of Scotland, the buildings were purchased by the Deeper Life Bible Church. However, the Romanian congregation retained the use of the church hall and continues to flourish.

49. RUCHILL KELVINSIDE PARISH CHURCH OF SCOTLAND
15–17, Shakespeare St, Maryhill, G20 8TH

In Glasgow, light-coloured sandstone was almost entirely used in construction until sources were depleted. Thereafter, red sandstone started to predominate until

Ruchill Kelvinside, shown above from the west, is situated very close to the late eighteenth-century Forth & Clyde Canal at Maryhill.

The hall is the more significant architecturally as it was designed by Charles Rennie Macintosh and is reminiscent of his Glasgow School of Art. It now functions as a tearoom.

bricks superseded it. At Ruchill the hall was built first, in 1899, of light sandstone. It operated as a mission for Westbourne Free Church (now Struthers Memorial Church) until a congregation formed a few years later as Ruchill United Free Church. The red-sandstone church was built in 1903–05.

50. SACRED HEART OF JESUS ROMAN CATHOLIC CHURCH
50 Old Dalmarnock Rd, Bridgeton, G40 4AU

Bridgeton did not exist until after Rutherglen Bridge was built in 1776 to facilitate trade between Rutherglen and Glasgow. This was a time when people were leaving the countryside and moving into towns where industrialisation was in its infancy and work was available. As in other places, Catholic immigrants from the Scottish Highlands and from Ireland continued to arrive in ever greater numbers in Glasgow and that included Bridgeton. Many Catholic Macdonalds from Glengarry found a home in Bridgeton.

The Sacred Heart started as a mission in 1873, initiated by St Mary's Parish in Calton, one of several which that church created. This was necessary to expand the church's support to its adherents in the areas where the Catholic population was expanding. Sacred Heart started as a temporary wooden church building in Old Dalmarnock Road which eventually ministered to an area as far east as Dalbeth.

A number of well-known artists and architects contributed to the decoration of this church. One lesser-known contributor was a First World War veteran whose

In 1910, the present red-sandstone basilica was opened, designed by Charles J. Menart. Above the entrance and beneath the Diocletian windows on the façade is the lettering 'Cordi Jesu Sacrum', translating from Latin as 'Sacred Heart of Jesus'.

life was saved when a bullet hit his chest but did not penetrate the prayer book in his tunic pocket. The book was gifted to the church in thanks for his miracle and it is occasionally displayed.

51. St Aloysius' Church – The Jesuit Church in the West of Scotland

25 Rose St, Garnethill, G3 6RE

A neck-stretching exercise is needed to take in this towering red-sandstone structure sitting on top of Garnethill.

The Jesuits arrived in Glasgow in 1859 and eventually built an iron and glass structure. It was nicknamed for Father Kay who came to the city in 1868 as 'Father Kay's Railway Shed' and was the St Aloysius parish church for forty years.

The design of the present church is by Charles J. Menart and opened in 1910, the same year as the Sacred Heart Church in Bridgeton by the same architect.

Ogilvie was born into a Calvinist family but while being educated in Europe as a teenager he converted to Catholicism. He joined the Society of Jesus in 1599 and was ordained a priest in 1610. Ogilvie returned to Scotland twice and on the second occasion was arrested and tortured to give the names of his associates,

St Aloysius, which
houses the National
Shrine of St John Ogilvie
(1579–1615).

which he refused to do. He was hanged and drawn at Glasgow Cross on 10 March 1615. As a martyr, Ogilvie was beatified in 1929.

The church of the Blessed St John Ogilvie was opened in 1960 in Easterhouse. Following the inexplicable overnight recovery from stomach cancer of a local parishioner, John Fagan, in 1967 it was declared miraculous through the intercession of the Blessed John Ogilvie. Consequently, he was canonised by Pope Paul VI on 17 October 1976. The church was renamed for St John Ogilvie. However, the congregation joined to that of St Jude's in Barlanark in 1980 and the church was demolished. In addition to the various artworks depicting St John Ogilvie in St Aloysius there is a painting by Peter Howson in St Andrew's RC Cathedral in Clyde St – the *Martyrdom of St John Ogilvie*.

52. ST ANDREW'S EAST PARISH CHURCH OF SCOTLAND
685 Alexandra Parade, Dennistoun, G31 3LN

This Dennistoun church originated from part of the congregation of St Andrew's Parish Church which left at the Disruption of 1843. At first, it worshipped in the ballroom of the Black Bull Hotel until it built a Free Church in North Hanover Street in 1844. In 1899, the congregation moved to a new church on Alexandra

The two churches of St Andrew's East, the smaller red-roofed building to the right being the original parish church and now restored to that capacity.

Parade in the east end of the city. This was Alexandra Park Free Church, named for the adjacent park. When the larger building was added to the west in 1903–04, the earlier was used as hall accommodation. As with many others it became a Church of Scotland in 1929 and acquired its present name. Sadly, the situation was reversed in 1996 when expensive repair work was required on the larger building. Eventually, it was sold and converted into flats. The hall was then refurbished and re-dedicated in April 2002 as the parish church. The two buildings remain a significant adornment to Alexandra Parade.

53. St Andrew's Parish Church of Scotland or St Andrew's in the Square
1 St Andrew's Square, Calton, G1 5PP

St Andrew's is one of the few remaining eighteenth-century buildings left in Glasgow. This burgh church was a jewel in the crown of Glasgow Presbytery for nearly 236 years and was the first completely new church to be built in Glasgow since the Reformation of 1560. The church was located just beyond the town boundary, on Eaglesham Croft, with the clear waters of the Molendinar Burn flowing nearby.

Above left and above right: Williamson et al. (1990) have described St Andrew's as 'the only building in Glasgow intact enough to display the taste and affluence of her Tobacco Lords', while the Listed Buildings records suggest it to be 'the most important and impressive 18th century church in Scotland'.

The construction took place over a surprisingly extended period, from 1739 to 1756, and was remarkably expensive. Its design by Alan Dreghorn very closely matches that of St Martin's-in-the-Field but has some quite different and notable features of its own to distinguish it from the London church.

The church has been the focus of several incidents of note. During its construction, the site provided some shelter to the ragged army of Prince Charles Edward Stuart during the winter of 1745–46 on its retreat from England. In 1784, the Italian aeronaut Vincent Lunardi demonstrated the first of his balloon ascents from St Andrew's in front of a crowd estimated to be in excess of 100,000.

An attempt was made to introduce organ music in the church on 23 August 1807, when an instrument previously owned by James Watt was played. However, the populace was outraged and it was never used there again.

At the Disruption of 1843, the Revd Nathaniel Paterson and 456 members of his congregation quit the building, leaving a mere thirty-five members to constitute St Andrew's. The church did eventually recover but the parish was then subject to a long-term decline in population as the result of slum clearance in its parish. Finally, in 1993, the congregation joined Calton New church to form St Luke's & St Andrew's in Calton, and St Andrew's was closed.

The building was sold to the Glasgow Building Preservation Trust in 1993, for the price of £1.00. It was leased to the St Andrew's in the Square Trust and was extensively restored to its former Baroque glory. The main hall was used as a centre for Scottish music, song and dance while the basement was excavated to provide a smaller and more informal venue, café and bistro known as Café Source. The lease was terminated in February 2020 and the building is currently for sale.

54. ST ANDREW'S ROMAN CATHOLIC METROPOLITAN CATHEDRAL
196 Clyde St, City Centre, G1 4JY

With the gradual reduction in the legal sanctions imposed against Catholicism and the influx of Catholic Irish and Highlanders, it was estimated by the second decade of the nineteenth century that there were around 3,000 Catholics in the

Above and below: This view of St Andrew's Cathedral on the north side of the River Clyde in 2020 is in contrast to Joseph Swan's engraving of the cathedral in 1828. The building's exterior has not changed significantly while the city around it certainly has.

Glasgow area. This led to the decision that a new and more commodious church be built. In 1816 St Andrew's Church opened. The Scottish Catholic hierarchy was restored in 1878, then came the first appointment of a Catholic Archbishop of Glasgow archdiocese since the Reformation. In 1889, after restoration work, the church became the cathedral of the archdiocese and in 1947, it became a metropolitan cathedral.

55. ST ANDREW'S WEST PARISH CHURCH OF SCOTLAND
260 Bath St, City Centre, G2 4JP

This Bath Street church was built in 1849–52 for some members of the George Street Congregational Church who had broken away. By 1874, the congregation had diminished and the building was sold, with the purchaser donating it to the Church of Scotland as Blythswood Parish Church. Over the years it would appear that there were fifteen congregational unions involving the building! In 1974, as Renfield Church of Scotland, it united with St Stephen's which had already been sharing the building, and became known as Renfield St Stephen's.

The church spire is a significant feature of the building. Given its age, the original was being repaired in 1998 when a severe storm caused it to collapse onto the church below causing major damage. It took the better part of three years to rebuild and it is reported that repairs cost around £3,000,000. Strangely enough, the storm occurred on Boxing Day, otherwise known as St Stephen's Day.

Recently, in 2019, the congregation of Anderson Kelvingrove joined that of Renfield St Stephen to form the new parish of St Andrew's West, taking the popular name of Scotland's patron saint.

56. ST ANNE'S ROMAN CATHOLIC CHURCH
21 Whitevale St, Dennistoun, G31 1QW

His biographer identifies similarities in the façade of St Anne's to the Chiesa Della Salute in Venice, and describes it as a building which was 'to herald a new approach

Another of Jack Coia's churches in the east end is St Anne's, which now provides a particular service to the local Polish community. It was his first commission for the Glasgow Archdiocese, in 1931, with it being completed in 1933.

The interior of St Anne's.

to church design in Scotland'. Coia was favoured by the Catholic Church in many subsequent projects. Among his other churches in Glasgow are St Columba of Iona's, Maryhill, St Paul's, Shettleston and Our Lady of Good Counsel's, Dennistoun.

57. ST ANTHONY'S ROMAN CATHOLIC CHURCH
62 Langlands Rd, Govan, G51 3BD

Built of blonde sandstone, St Anthony's is pierced by windows with the typical Romanesque arches as opposed to the pointed Gothic. There are coloured bands and stripes in pink stone throughout the exterior. The bell tower – or campanile as it is also called – is surmounted by a pyramid-shaped spire. Sadly, the northern façade is partially covered for summertime repairs, but even with this there are enough of the features of the church on view to appreciate it – a touch of Italy in Govan!

Built to a design by John Honeyman from 1877 to 1879, St Anthony's is quite unusual for the period as a example of Italian Romanesque architecture.

58. St Benedict's Roman Catholic Church

755 Westerhouse Rd, Easterhouse, G34 9RP

Prior to the building of the housing estate from the mid-1950s, Easterhouse had largely been a rural area, rather exposed to the weather and isolated on the periphery of the city. To make matters more difficult, remarkably few community resources had been included for the residents in Glasgow's plans, which resulted in a great many problems for the residents as well as for the city. For many years some gaps were filled by the churches which were located to the area.

Above is the renovated St Benedict's with spacious interior shown left.

St Benedict's is one of a pair of churches which now make up the St John Bosco Parish in Easterhouse, the other being St Clare's. The original parish was founded in 1958 but for the first year people had to travel to St Bridget's in Baillieston for services. Thereafter, with the opening of St Benedict's primary school, this temporarily met their requirements. It was not until 1965 that St Benedict's Church was opened. By the arrival of the new millennium in 2000 St Benedict's was already showing some age, so the old buildings were extensively renovated, with the work completed by 2005.

59. ST CHARLES OF BORROMEO ROMAN CATHOLIC ORATORY
1 Kelvinside Gardens, North Kelvinside, G20 6BG

St Charles was built from 1959–60 to an original design by Jack Coia and further developed by Andy MacMillan and Isi Metzstein of Gillespie, Kidd & Coia. At the time it is said to have become well known throughout Scotland. It was built on an awkward site, on a steep slope to the south and blocked by a stone stairway to the east. It was framed in reinforced concrete and in-filled by brickwork. The vaulted roof was also in concrete, as was the free-standing 80-foot-high bell tower in the church's piazza. The interior has several innovative and very interesting features which include some work of the sculptor Benno Schotz such as the statuary of the *Stations of the Cross*. Each church decides how it represents these and St Charles does so quite strikingly. Both Schotz and Coia are depicted among the sixty-four terracotta figures which make up a 3-foot-high frieze.

St Charles of Borromeo – a controversial and innovative design.

The architecture of this church must have been subjected to a fair amount of controversy at its completion. It was innovative for its time and it certainly can make the viewer stop and consider what their opinion is beyond the immediate. In the first instance, I see the exterior of the church as industrial in appearance – like a large factory with a chimney stack, out of context with the surrounding buildings – probably because I have worked in large factories built in the same materials. The separate bell tower seems remarkably stark. Nevertheless, this does not mean this church should not have been built, because there will be many who see its intrinsic worth and its aspirations. It is in the nature of architecture to push the frontiers of innovation, otherwise we would end up with the tedious and uninspiring.

60. St Columba Gaelic Church of Scotland Fàilte gu Eaglais Ghàidhlig Chaluim Cille

300 St Vincent St, City Centre, G2 5RU

Gaelic churches of various denominations eventually started to appear, such St Columba Gaelic Church of Scotland and Partick Free Gaelic Church (now Glasgow Reformed Presbyterian Church).

Although Glasgow had Gaelic speakers in churches from at least the late seventeenth century, it was with the exponential growth of industry from the eighteenth century onwards that attracted large numbers of Gaelic speakers to the city. Communities were formed as one would expect and, since many did not speak English, more church services needed to be in Gaelic.

St Columba's started in the city centre as early as 1770 when the Ingram Street Gaelic Chapel was opened in Back Cow Loan. In 1837 it was sold for a very good price (£12,000) which enabled it to build the Hope Street church in 1824. This was eventually lost to the construction of the Central railway station but with the financial compensation received the present St Columba's was built in 1902–04. The poet Duncan Livingstone carved the inscription 'Tigh Mo Chridhe, Tigh Mo Gràidh' ('House of My Heart, House of My Love') on the lintel of the main door of the church. The church is sometimes referred to as the Gaelic Cathedral.

Although some of the immigrants may eventually have returned to their original homes, many of their children would probably not do so. Their aspirations would now differ from their parents and they would be changed in many other ways because of their new environment. Most would probably learn English, would acquire English-speaking friends and marry outside of their Highland communities. They would embrace a new lifestyle and the need for Gaelic-speaking churches would diminish.

61. ST COLUMBA OF IONA ROMAN CATHOLIC CHURCH
74 Hopehill Rd, Maryhill, G20 7HH

St Columba's has written its own story of the church on a wall plaque:

This church was completed in 1941, during the 2nd World War and during the Blitz in Govan and Clydebank. The original Church was in Cameron Street which is now demolished and the architecture of this new Church was by Gillespie, Kidd and Coia. In recent years it has been listed as a 'Grade A' building. The imposing west front of the church is Italian Romanesque in inspiration. At the time it was built this area was densely populated and the parish had a huge congregation. Each of the red bricks of the building were paid for – at 6 pence a time – by families in the parish. The painted panels of the Stations of the Cross inside were by Hugh Adam Crawford, transferred from the Empire Exhibition in Bellahouston Park (1938) and the Crucifix behind the High Altar is by the artist Benno Schotz.

St Columba (*c.* 521–597) is possibly the most famous saint of the Celtic Christian Church which preceded the Roman Catholic Church in Scotland. The Celtic Church structure was largely based on monastic inter-relationship rather than the hierarchical system favoured by the Catholic Church. He founded the famous community on the island of Iona but also travelled around what was to become Scotland. He is credited with laying the foundation for Pictland's conversion to Christianity.

62. ST GEORGE'S IN THE FIELDS CHURCH OF SCOTLAND
485 St George's Rd, Woodside, G3 6JX

The original church of St George's in the Fields was built *c.* 1832 in Woodside at a time when the area was still a very rural location – hence its name. Glasgow has made several attempts to develop this area but plans do not seem to have fully achieved its intentions. The southern part of the road is quite bleak as it passes beside and under the motorway. However, the northern stretch has at least two significant buildings – Carnegie's Woodside Library and the current second version of the church. The latter was built in 1885–86, similar to Wellington Church of Scotland and of approximately the same period – yet another of Glasgow's favoured Greek Temples! The building was converted into flats in 1988–89.

It is most likely that this church eventually gave its name to nearby St George's Cross and St George's Road.

One of Glasgow city centre's iconic churches is St George's Tron which sits in Nelson Mandela Place with its eastern façade dominating George Street. It was built from 1807–09 to a design by William Stark and was originally known as the West Church. This was because it was built at a place which, at that time, marked Glasgow's western boundary.

63. ST GEORGE'S TRON CHURCH OF SCOTLAND
163 Buchanan St, City Centre, G1

Splits in congregations over matters of ideology are not uncommon in all denominations, especially when social norms progress more rapidly than some churches would like. Such issues arise more rapidly nowadays and there is a greater opportunity for them to be considered by a wider audience given the technology now available.

In 2012, St George's experienced such an event when the issue arose of whether or not ministers in same sex relationships within the Church of Scotland was acceptable. As a consequence, the serving minister and the entire congregation seceded from the Church of Scotland and departed rather than accept this. Nevertheless, St George's Tron survived and was transformed by its new minister, Revd Alastair Duncan, and his support workers. It continues to recover and provides a valuable and inspired service to a city centre parish population whether transient or permanent.

64. ST HELEN'S ROMAN CATHOLIC CHURCH
32 Langside Avenue, Shawlands, G41 2QS

This area of Glasgow was acquired by the city in 1857 with Queen's Park being developed and opened in 1862. The large recreational area was named for Mary, Queen of Scots and in memory of her defeat in the Battle of Langside in 1568. The peripheral areas of the park were allocated for building.

St Helen's faces across a busy main road into the park. It was originally built for the United Presbyterian Church of Scotland in 1896–97 and was named Langside Avenue. The exterior is of two colours of stonework, the main surfaces built with what is described as yellow-snecked rubble. The dressings are of red ashlar. The eastern entrance was supposed to have been surmounted by a tower and spire, but this did not materialise.

St Helen was a British princess born (*c*. AD 250–*c*. AD 330) and was buried in Rome. She had married a Roman officer and their son became the Emperor Constantine, the first Christian Emperor. She was involved in excavations on Mount Calvary where three crosses were uncovered in a ditch. These were taken to be the crosses of the Crucifixion. A dying woman was placed on each cross to try to determine which was that of Jesus. On one she recovered and this was taken to be a miracle indicating the True Cross.

With subsequent denominational unions, St Helen's eventually became a Church of Scotland in 1929. In time, with two other fellow churches nearby resulting in a surplus of accommodation, its congregation joined that of Shawlands, forming Shawlands Old, in 1963. This provided an opportunity for the Catholic Church to provide a much-needed local church. The building was successfully acquired and was opened in 1966 for the Catholics of Langside and Shawlands.

65. ST JOHN THE EVANGELIST SCOTTISH EPISCOPAL CHURCH
21 Swinton Rd, Baillieston, G69 6DS

St John's is the oldest Scottish Episcopal Church building in Glasgow still being used for its original purpose. It was built in 1850 on the initiative of local coalmasters whose concern for their employees' spiritual welfare seems to have far exceeded any interest in their physical well-being.

Like other churches, St John's has also had to struggle through the years to keep up its membership role. A story associated with the church concerned a diocesan committee assessment in 1908 to determine whether or not St John's was still viable.

Reminiscent of the film *The Quiet Man*, the priest of St Bridget's Roman Catholic Church next door exhorted his congregation to attend St John's when the bishop came one Sunday morning. The bishop was so impressed at the turnout that St John's was saved.

66. St John's Renfield Church of Scotland
22 Beaconsfield Rd, G12 0NY

Situated on an elevated site, the approach from the south-west provides a superb view of this imposing and attractive structure. The bright interior reflects the relative simplicity of the exterior design. It is quite outstanding and reminiscent of a cathedral rather than a parish church. It was dedicated in 1931, the congregation having moved west from their church in the city centre.

St Jude's Free Presbyterian was built in 1874–75 as Woodlands Road United Presbyterian Church. This view is taken from a postcard dated around 1907.

67. St Jude's Free Presbyterian Church
137 Woodlands Rd, Woodlands, G3 6LE

The surroundings have not changed significantly apart from how quiet the street looks compared to the heavy traffic of the present day. This church's history provides some idea of the complexity of the background of many of Glasgow's churches.

The builders of this beautiful A listed structure have a legacy going back to the east end of Glasgow and the Anti-Burgher side of the split in the Secession Church of 1747. The congregation eventually became part of the United Presbyterian Church, then of the United Free Church and finally of the Church of Scotland, through the various denominational unions over the years. As Woodlands Church of Scotland, the congregation eventually quit its building when it joined the Wellington Church of Scotland in University Avenue in 1974.

The following year the congregation of St Jude's Free Presbyterian Church in West George Street took possession of the building and is still there. Some stained glass and the organ were removed from the church as a condition of the purchase since these features were not consistent with the new congregation's beliefs. However, these items were eventually used elsewhere or stored.

68. Saint Luke's/St Luke's & St Andrew's Parish Church of Scotland
17 Bain Square, Calton, G40 2JZ

Calton developed into an independent burgh on the lands of Blackfauld, adjacent to Glasgow's eastern boundary. With its own burgh hall and police force, it retained its independence until it was incorporated into Glasgow in 1846. St Luke's & St Andrew's, originally St Luke's, was built in 1836–37 in what was then Calton's Main Street. It was initially a chapel of ease to the Barony parish then became a parish church in its own right in 1863.

St Luke's is now a favoured alternative music venue. Happily, the interior of the building has been preserved to a significant extent.

St Luke's experience of the Disruption of 1843 was repeated over the whole of Scotland. Most of the St Luke's congregation joined the new Free Church but retained the building for six years before being forced to leave following a House of Lord's decision as to the Church of Scotland's property rights. The donor of St Luke's clocks had them removed to be used in a new Free Church when it was available.

After 1961, with a significant fall in membership in all churches due to the removal of inner-city inhabitants to various housing schemes from the 1950s, St Luke's gradually absorbed no less than ten other local congregations. It became Calton New from 1961 to 1992 and then gained its final designation when the St Andrew's Parish Church congregation joined.

St Luke's & St Andrew's itself finally closed but in around 2013 the property was purchased and converted into a venue for music, arts and other events – Saint Luke's.

69. St Margaret's Church of Scotland
100 Polmadie Rd, Polmadie, G42 0PH

The district of Polmadie is believed to have been named from the Gaelic for 'the little pool or stream haunted by savage dogs or wolves'. The burn is still in existence, running through Richmond Park, and not far from St Margaret's.

One of Govan Parish's many 'daughter' churches, St Margaret's was started as a mission from Govan in 1897 and opened in 1902.

This B listed church, hall and manse is an escapee from the mass demolition and reconstruction of the Gorbals/Oatlands/Polmadie areas of the city south of the River Clyde. It stands alone, looking abandoned and in a rather dilapidated condition, surrounded by modern housing. It closed in 1984 and is now owned by Glasgow City Council. Hopefully a use can be found for this little survivor of 118 years, to help preserve an area so denuded of historical interest.

70. ST MARY OF THE ASSUMPTION ROMAN CATHOLIC CHURCH
89 Abercromby St, Calton, G40 2DG

St Mary's was opened on 15 August 1842. It was the second chapel to be erected in Glasgow since the Reformation of 1560, the first being what is now St Andrew's RC Metropolitan Cathedral. In 1839 Bishop Scott authorised Revd Peter Forbes to solicit alms in Ireland to build churches in the west of Scotland. His efforts were highly successful and he was placed in charge of the new mission in Calton which extended from there to Coatbridge. This area of responsibility was reduced

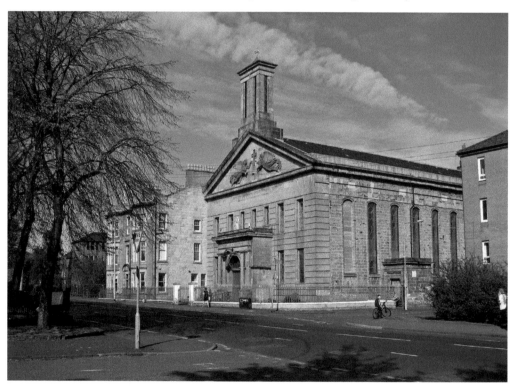

My own father had an interesting story of when he was a soldier in the Second World War. He was stationed in Italy for a time and met Pope Pius XII at the Vatican. He asked my father where he was from and was told Bridgeton. The Pope said he knew the area well as he had worked at St Mary's very early in his career! I have tried to verify this at St Mary's and the Vatican but there is no evidence. However, the Vatican did advise that it was certainly possible as not all records of the Pope's early actions were kept or even made. Decide for yourselves!

over the years as subsequent missions, such as Sacred Heart, were established. Revd Forbes died in 1872 and was interred beneath the Sacred Heart Chapel of St Mary's. The street to the south of the chapel bears his name.

St Mary's has a very close connection to Celtic Football Club. Brother Walfrid of the Marist Order was particularly involved in establishing football teams for the local Catholic boys, and proposed the name of 'Celtic' when that particular team was being formed.

71. ST MARY'S SCOTTISH EPISCOPAL CATHEDRAL
300 Great Western Rd, Woodside, G4 9JB

The history of some of the earlier Scottish Episcopal congregations can be quite obscure. They were not generally well regarded after appearing to have supported the Jacobite rebellions of 1715 and 1745. As a result, they tended towards keeping a low profile or maintaining actual secrecy. The origin of the congregation of St Mary itself remains vague. It has been suggested to have been formed as early as 1688, but no proof has been shown. More realistically, it is reckoned to have emerged by around 1750 at the latest.

The new St Mary's was opened in 1871 but the spire was not added until 1893. The main design was provided by George Gilbert Scott (or more likely by an associate) but was not wholly satisfying to many who saw it as largely a copy of others he had built. However, it would be unusual if everybody agreed about the outcome of such a project. In 1908 St Mary's was designated as the cathedral for the diocese of Glasgow & Galloway.

In 1804 the Scottish Episcopal Church accepted the Hanoverian succession, so the need for some level of reticence or secrecy seems to have dissipated by 1825 when St Mary's Episcopal Chapel opened in Renfield Street – at that time quite a well-to-do residential area. As time passed however, the area deteriorated and became more commercialised. Those of the congregation who could afford to started to move further west. It was eventually decided that the church be sold when a new one had been built at a site found on Great Western Road, at Woodside.

72. ST MICHAEL'S ROMAN CATHOLIC CHURCH
1350 Gallowgate, Parkhead, G31 4DJ

St Michael's is situated on one of Glasgow's most famous streets – the Gallowgate, near Parkhead Cross. At the turn of the nineteenth century Parkhead was still a small village. However, it grew rapidly to become a worldwide industrial giant with the growth of the original Parkhead Forge. Sadly, with the loss of industry and other local businesses, it is now experiencing something of an economic decline.

A Catholic mission in Parkhead was established in 1876 at the instigation of St Mary's in Calton. Initially, a school with a chapel included was built in Nisbet Street. It served the community until the construction of a separate, temporary church was finally achieved in 1900 at Nisbet Street's junction with Salamanca Street. This temporary measure lasted much longer than anticipated – for sixty-nine years! The present – and permanent – St Michael's Church was not opened until 1969.

Above and right: A notable feature of the church's exterior is a tapered brick pier on the east end of the building, surmounted by a statue of the church's namesake, St Michael the Archangel.

73. ST PAUL THE APOSTLE ROMAN CATHOLIC CHURCH
1653 Shettleston Rd, Shettleston, G32 9AR

St Paul's also started as a mission in 1850, initiated by St Mary's RC Church in the Calton. It was housed in a wooden hut in Eastmuir at first, serving a very large area. A stone church followed in 1857 which lasted 102 years, to be replaced by the present St Paul's which was built from 1957 to 1959. It is another of Jack Coia's designs and described as one of the 'last basilican churches' undertaken by the firm of Gillespie, Kidd & Coia.

The most notable feature of the church's exterior is the tower with large figures of the Crucifixion by the artist Jack Mortimer.

St Paul's interior.

St Rollox is the most recent of churches to be built in Glasgow. It resulted from the demolition of its church during the current regeneration of the Sighthill district by Glasgow City Council.

74. ST ROLLOX PARISH CHURCH OF SCOTLAND
70 Fountainwell Rd, Sighthill, G21 1RG

St Rollox is a misnomer for its medieval predecessor, the chapel of St Roche the Confessor. The chapel was built in *c.* 1508 on moorland to the north of the town which was part of Glasgow Cathedral's domain. A number of chapels were distributed throughout the latter's properties for various purposes apart from worship, such as tending the sick.

St Roche was popularly invoked for protection against plague and the chapel had a cemetery which might have been used for the victims of deadly infections. Those thought to have become infected are believed to have been driven from the town onto this moorland, possibly to seek sanctuary at the chapel.

The new church, which opened in 2019, is of a very modern design, unique to the city. Its two wings join at an entrance rotunda to form a 'V' shape structure. It incorporates separate spaces for a variety of activities for the community in addition to the sanctuary within the south wing. The members of the Sighthill congregation are diverse in their origins, forming a multi-cultural group which provides support to both the church and each other.

The regeneration of the area is still underway. Given how densely populated and industrialised this part of Glasgow was around fifty years ago, it is remarkable to see such a wide-open space in Sighthill just now, a sight possibly not seen since the original church was there.

75. ST SIMON'S ROMAN CATHOLIC CHURCH
33 Partick Bridge St, Partick, G11 6PQ

St Simon's was built in 1858 and is the third oldest Catholic church in Glasgow, after St Andrew's Cathedral and St Mary's RC Church. It was initially called

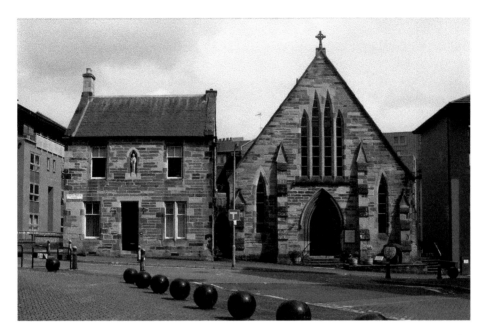

Above: St Simon's RC.

Right: The plaques outside the church's entrance.

St Peter's but when a new and larger St Peter's was built in Hyndland Street in 1903 it was renamed as Bridge Street Church. From 1940 to 1943 it was called the Polish Church as Polish troops in Yorkhill Barracks attended every Sunday. In 1945 it took the name of St Simon, from the Apostle Simon Peter.

After the war, the Poles who remained in the city continued to use St Simon's. Since then, many others have come to Glasgow from the European Union, adding to the Cosmopolitan feel of the city. While St Simon's and St Peter's continue to provide services, St Anne's RC Church in Dennistoun has also been formalised as a church for the Polish community.

The extent to which the Poles appreciated the support shown them during the war is indicated in the two copies of plaques at the entrance to St Simon's. One shows the Black Madonna, and the other has an inscription:

> 1939–1945 – during the Second World War Polish soldiers, on leave from the battlefields, came to this church to attend mass together, to hear the word of God in their native tongue, to sing their Polish hymns, and to thank Our Lady, Queen of Poland. For this touch of home the Polish community of Glasgow has, through the years, felt deeply grateful to father Patrick Tierney for the privilege he has accorded them of celebrating the Polish mass in this church and for the many kindnesses received from him and the parishioners – 'I was a stranger and you took me in.'

To the present day, the church contains a painting of the Black Madonna of Częstochowa – Queen and Protectress of Poland at the Lady Altar – a gift of the Polish Army.

76. SHAWLANDS OLD CHURCH OF SCOTLAND
1120 Pollokshaws Rd, Shawlands, G41 3QP

Local residents asked for a mission in the Shawlands area with a view to establishing a Church of Scotland congregation and church there. The application

This rather imposing building resulted from a request by some residents of Shawlands to the Presbytery of Paisley within which authority the district lay until 1929.

was successful and a wooden church was initially provided in 1877 with a permanent building opening in 1889. It became Shawlands Parish Church in 1901. In 1963 it was joined by the congregation of the Langside Avenue, now St Helen's RC Church, to be renamed as Shawlands Old. This united congregation removed in 1998 to join Shawlands Cross, which is now Shawlands Trinity Church. The building has been used by a number of other denominations in subsequent years.

77. SHAWLANDS TRINITY PARISH CHURCH OF SCOTLAND
5 Moss Side Rd, Shawlands, G41 3TP

Shawlands Trinity started as a Free Church in 1898 in a hall at Shawlands Cross, taking the location's name. The present building was completed in 1903. It participated in the denominational unions which took place in 1900 and 1929, eventually becoming an Established Church provision.

Until 1963 there were still three congregations in very close proximity to Shawlands Cross, a situation that became untenable. Two united in 1963 to form Shawlands Old and in 1998 the latter united to Shawlands Cross to become simply Shawlands. Finally (so far) it was also joined by South Shawlands in 2017 (now RE-HOPE Southside) when it took its current name of Shawlands Trinity.

The landmark Shawlands Trinity Church at Shawlands Cross.

78. SPRINGBURN PARISH CHURCH OF SCOTLAND
180 Springburn Way, Springburn, G21 1TU

Springburn Hill Church was dedicated in 1842 as a chapel of ease *quoad sacra* (i.e., with limited authority) to the Barony parish. It became fully independent in 1854 as Springburn Parish Church, *quoad omnia* (i.e., with full authority) in 1854.

As with many districts in or around Glasgow in the nineteenth century, Springburn became a heavily populated and industrialised area. Glasgow's authorities eventually felt the need to implement a major regeneration plan in the 1970s which changed the whole face of Springburn, leaving it almost unrecognisable.

Left is an image of the original Springburn church from a postcard of *c.* 1914. Above is the replacement building of 1981.

The requirements of the Glasgow authorities included extensive demolition in Springburn which meant the removal of various churches, including the historic Springburn church. There then followed years of complex and protracted negotiations which finally ended in an agreement.

The final plan was to gradually consolidate the eight churches involved and then provide a single new church for the resulting congregation. The closed buildings would be transferred to Glasgow for demolition. The new church, opened in May 1981, was named Springburn Parish Church.

79. STRATHBUNGO CHURCH OF SCOTLAND
603 Pollokshaws Rd, Strathbungo, G41 2QA

The district of Strathbungo developed from a small village known as Marchtown, situated at the junction of the Church of Scotland parishes of Govan and Cathcart. March is an old Scots word for a boundary or frontier. Mission work started there in 1833 with a church being built in 1839. The latter was noted by Hugh Macdonald in his 1854 book *Rambles Around Glasgow*, as was a description of the village which seems to have been small but with its fair share of pubs.

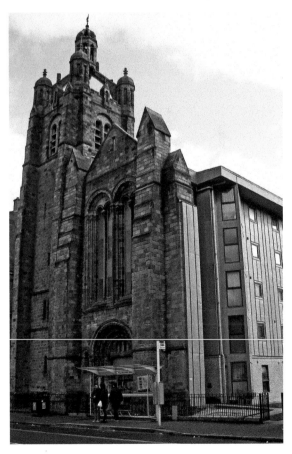

Strathbungo church converted to housing.

The church became Strathbungo Parish Church in 1879 and was replaced in 1886, incorporating some of the original materials. In 1979 the congregation joined with Queen's Park West and the building was sold to be used for educational purposes by the local Pakistani community. The body of the church was eventually demolished. However, the entrance façade and tower were saved and incorporated into a new housing block to the rear, creating a very interesting hybrid.

80. STRUTHERS MEMORIAL PENTECOSTAL CHURCH
52 Westbourne Gardens, Hyndland, G12 9XF

The current occupant of the Westbourne Gardens building was founded in the 1950s by Elizabeth Taylor and Hugh B. Black, and was initially known as the Independent Pentecostal Church. Their first church building was located in Greenock and was a vacant Reformed Presbyterian Church.

The building was designed by John Honeyman and built between 1880–81 as Westbourne Free Church. It had started as the Western Road Free Church in an iron church, a temporary measure used by many churches to facilitate the development of new congregations. Over the years Westbourne was instrumental in forming satellite missions to help develop fully fledged congregations. Part of its legacy is Ruchill Kelvinside Church.

Westbourne was joined by the congregation of the Belhaven Church in 1960, which is now the Greek Orthodox Cathedral of St Luke the Evangelist Scotland in Dundonald Road. It ended in 1990 as Belhaven Westbourne Church of Scotland.

This church was named in memory of Glasgow-born Revd John Paterson Struthers (1851–1915), a very well-respected minister in the Reformed Presbyterian Church and children's author. His name has been carried over to this Glasgow church.

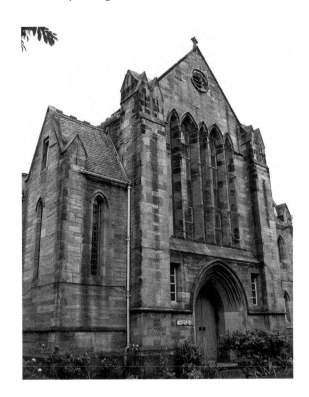

This unmistakably ecclesiastical building is presently used as a residential care home for older people.

81. Swinton Hill Care Home/Mure Memorial Church of Scotland

150 Swinton Rd, Swinton, G69 6DW

This care home was built in Swinton in 1882 as the Mure Memorial Miners' Free Church, reflecting its historical connection with the miners of the wider Baillieston district. The original congregation was founded in nearby West Maryston village where it went under a number of names, including the Children's Church and the Miners' Church. The Swinton congregation eventually moved to a new home built in Garrowhill where it continues to this day as the Mure Memorial Church of Scotland.

The Swinton building was acquired by the Roman Catholic Church in the late 1940s for use as a home for the elderly named St Catherine's House. The home was ultimately transferred to private ownership, to become Swinton Hill Care Home, with one of the conditions of the sale being that the small chapel within the main building be retained as a sanctuary for the use of the residents.

82. Townhead & Blochairn Parish Church of Scotland
176 Royston Hill, Roystonhill, G21 2LN

Sitting atop Roystonhill is this survivor of the Townhead & Blochairn church. With the addition of its own considerable height to that of the hill it sits upon, the tower and spire are a landmark that can be seen from a considerable distance.

The church was built in 1865–66 and started life as Townhead Parish Church. Towards the end of the twentieth century it was decided that the life of the building had run its course and had to be taken down. However, the tower and spire were preserved and the remaining land used to form a small park called Spire Park.

83. TRINITY METHODIST CHURCH
1104 Shettleston Rd, Shettleston, G32 7PH

The establishment of Methodism in Shettleston is said to have resulted largely from the efforts of one man, William Brown, who was converted at a prayer meeting and thereafter attended the Tollcross Methodist Church. He lived in Shettleston, and determined that a Primitive Methodist chapel should be built for the inhabitants of that rapidly developing district.

Over the years it provided a haven to some of those Methodists displaced from other societies which have ceased to exist, such as St Thomas' in Gallowgate and Waddell Memorial in Parkhead. With the closure of the Tollcross Church in 1976, Trinity became the only remaining Methodist church in the east end of the city.

Eventually, the society was faced with the usual need to meet the repair and maintenance costs for a 118-year-old building, as well as the reduction in membership to meet these costs. It was finally sold in early 2020, just prior to

Through Brown's efforts, a temporary 'Tin Tabernacle' was built in Shettleston in 1889. It lasted beyond the anticipated ten years of its projected lifespan until the society had become sufficiently well established to build a permanent structure. Built in blonde sandstone, it opened for worship on New Year's Day, 1902.

the Covid-19 pandemic, and its future use remains unknown. However, the membership has not dissolved but holds Sunday services in the local Salvation Army hall. They also meet at a variety of other settings including their homes. The spirit of William Brown remains in the east end.

84. TRIRATNA (GLASGOW) BUDDHIST CENTRE
329 Sauchiehall St, G2 3HW

Buddhism has become increasingly popular in western countries. The Glasgow Centre is located in the heart of the city. In a tenement on the very busy Sauchiehall Street it provides a welcome haven of tranquillity. The Centre originates from the Friends of the Western Buddhist Order which was founded in 1967 and was renamed the Triratna Buddhist Order in 2010. The founder was Urgyen Sangharakshita (1925–2018), formerly Dennis Longwood. He remained in India after the Second World War when he was demobilised from the British Army and subsequently practised Buddhism for twenty years before returning to London where he established the Order.

The Glasgow Centre for the Buddhist community provides classes in Buddhism and meditation.

The shrine room, where meditation takes place, contains a statue of the Buddha on a raised and decorated plinth. Triratna is a Sanskrit term meaning 'Three Jewels' – Buddha (the Enlightened One), Dharma (Teachings) and Sangha (Community).

85. Tron Theatre/Tron St Mary's Church of Scotland
63 Trongate, City Centre, G1 5HB

Originally built as a collegiate church, St Mary & St Anne's was founded in *c*. 1484. After the Reformation of 1560 it fell into decline, but fortunately was rebuilt in *c*. 1592 as a city, or burgh, church of which there were only ever ten to serve the town over the years. These ten were eventually supported by additional churches at need as the population grew beyond the old town limits and their parishes.

In time St Mary's & St Anne's became known by several names such as the Laigh Kirk (i.e., Scots for Low Church) while the cathedral was the High Church. At one point, the church was known as the Tron Church or Tron Kirk simply because it stored a public tron – a weighing apparatus – in the base of its steeple. This was used to check the weight of imports into the town so that appropriate taxes could be levied.

The church survived Glasgow's Great Fires of 1652 and 1677 but did not avoid the disastrous mischief of some members of the local Hellfire Club in 1793. One night, they managed to gain access to a part of the church that was used as a guardhouse. With the guards out on patrol, the members managed to cause a disastrous fire which destroyed the session house and the church. Only the steeple survived – as it has to this day. A replacement church was built the following year, although it was not actually attached to the old steeple, and became known as Tron St Mary's. In 1855 the base of the steeple was pierced with arches to facilitate pedestrians walking on a pavement through it rather than round it.

The one-time medieval church of St Mary's at Glasgow Cross, now the Tron Theatre.

By 1946 the city centre population had diminished greatly and could no longer support most of the old churches, so some were vacated. Many of Tron St Mary's congregation had moved to Balornock and had used a temporary hall as Balornock Tron until a new church was built in 1965. At that time, it took the name of the old church, Tron St Mary's. In 1980 the old building was leased by Glasgow to the Glasgow Theatre Club and was subsequently converted to become the Tron Theatre.

86. WEBSTER'S THEATRE/LANSDOWNE CHURCH OF SCOTLAND
416 Great Western Rd, Kelvinbridge, G4 9HZ

Lansdowne was designed by John Honeyman in the Gothic Revival style and built in 1862–64 as a United Presbyterian Church. The spire was believed to be the highest in the city (if not in Europe) rising 218 feet. Beyond Lansdowne can be seen the spire of St Mary's Scottish Episcopal Cathedral.

Lansdowne originated from the Cambridge Steet UP church when a group of sixty-three of the wealthier members decided to have a church further to the west. They, and the minister, Dr Eadie, left Cambridge Street in 1863. The move does not appear to have been appreciated by all of Cambridge's congregation with the following being chalked onto the wall of the new church:

> This church is not for the poor and needy,
> but for the rich and Dr Eadie.
> The rich may come in and take their seat,
> but the poor go on to Cambridge Street.

Lansdowne eventually experienced the same challenges as many others and, with a decline in its congregation, it finally merged with nearby Kelvin Stevenson Memorial Church in 2014 to form Kelvinbridge Parish Church of Scotland. The A listed premises are now occupied by Webster's Theatre.

This view eastwards from the Kelvin Bridge along Great Western Road is from a postcard of *c.* 1907. Two earlier bridges over the river were replaced by this grander crossing in 1891. Just beyond the bridge is what was then Lansdowne United Free Church.

87. WELLINGTON CHURCH OF SCOTLAND
77 Southpark Ave, Hillhead, G12 8LE

Sitting on an elevated site within the campus of Glasgow University, this church is prominent even amongst many other notable buildings. Its southern façade of a Corinthian column-lined portico faces into University Avenue. It was built from 1882–84 on the site of Oakfield House for a United Presbyterian congregation which previously had a church in Wellington Street from 1827 (Wellington Street Church). The latter had a crypt to deter the activities of the resurrectionists of the period. However, given a continuing deterioration in its surroundings from the depletion of the immediate population and the increase of industrial and commercial development, the church's crypt was emptied and the building was sold. The congregation moved west and is now part of the Church of Scotland.

In 1974 the congregation of the Woodlands church (now St Jude's Free Presbyterian Church) joined with Wellington. Curiously, both congregations had their origin in the Havannah/Duke St Anti-Burgher Church in the east end of Glasgow with Wellington's descendants separating in 1792. Its subsequent history also mirrors much of St Jude's in terms of reunions with separated denominations over the centuries.

The name of the church has an obvious source – the Iron Duke who is recalled in a variety of memorials throughout Glasgow, not least for his statue with the almost permanent parking bollard on his head. From the sublime to the ridiculous?

SELECTED BIBLIOGRAPHY

Cameron, Nigel M. de S., et al. (1993), *Dictionary of Scottish Church History & Theology*, Edinburgh, T & T Ltd

Fisher, Joe (1994), *The Glasgow Encyclopedia*, Edinburgh, Mainstream Publishing Company

Gordon, J. S. F. (1872), *Glasghu Facies*, Glasgow, John Tweed (also known as *Glasgow Ancient & Modern*)

Herron, Andrew (1984) & Wale, Andrew (2007), *Historical Directory to Glasgow Presbytery*, Glasgow Presbytery (available online)

Levy, A. (1949), *The Origins of Glasgow Jewry 1812-1895*, Glasgow, A. J. MacFarlane Ltd

MacDonald, Ian R. (1995), *Glasgow's Gaelic Churches*, Edinburgh, The Knox Press

Rogerson, Robert W. K. C. (1986), *Jack Coia, His Life and Work*, Glasgow, R. W. K. C. Rogerson

White, Gavin (1998), *The Scottish Episcopal Church – A New History*, General Synod of the Scottish Episcopal Church

Williamson, E., Riches, A. & Higgs, M. (1990), *The Buildings of Scotland – Glasgow*, London, Penguin Books

IMAGE SOURCES

The following images are reproduced by the consent of the following copyright owners:

© Adams Gordon; 2, 3, 7(1), 7(2), 8, 9, 11(1), 11(2), 14, 15, 16(1), 16(2), 17(1), 17(2), 19, 20, 21, 25, 26, 28, 30(1), 31, 32(1) 33, 37, 40, 41, 46, 47, 48(1), 48(2), 49(2), 51, 52(1), 54(1), 55, 57, 58(1), 58(2), 60, 62, 64, 65, 68, 69, 71, 73(1), 73(2), 77, 78(1), 80, 81, 83, 87

© O'Connor, Gary; 1(1), 4, 5, 10(1), 10(2), 12(2), 12(3), 13, 18(1), 18(2), 22, 23, 24(1), 24(2), 27, 29(1), 34, 35, 36, 38, 39, 42, 43, 45(1), 45(2), 50(1), 53(2), 56(1), 56(2), 59, 61, 63, 66, 70, 72(1), 72(2), 74, 75(1), 75(2), 76, 79, 82(1), 84, 85(1)

© O'Donnell, Sam; Adelaide Pl, 1(2)

Queen's Cross – © dave souza – Own Work / Wikimedia Commons. Used under CC BY-SA 4.0 licence. – 44

Ruchill Church – © dave souza – Own Work / Wikimedia Commons. Used under CC BY-SA 4.0 licence. – 49(1)

St Andrew's Parish Church – © User: Colin / Wikimedia Commons. Used under CC BY-SA 4.0 licence. 53(1)

St Luke's Greek Cathedral – © Atgets Apprentice / Wikimedia Commons. Used under CC BY-SA 4.0 licence. – 32(2)

Unknown; 6, 12(1), 17(1), 29(2), 30(2), 54(2), 67, 78(2), 86

Acknowledgements

My thanks to all who have helped to make this book possible, especially during particularly difficult times:

Adelaide Pl – Sam O'Donnell
Bridgeton St Francis, etc. – Revd Howard Hudson
Calton Parkhead – Revd Alison Davidge
Glasgow Cathedral – Michelle Anderson, Historic Environment Scotland
St Kentigern's – Fr Jim Benton-Evans
Glasgow Hindu Mandir – Andrew Lal
Glasgow Royal Infirmary – Anne MacDonald
St Luke's Greek Orthodox Cathedral – Noncas Pitticas
Romanian Orthodox – Deacon Clyde Ross
Sacred Heart – Mon Paul M. Conroy
St Andrew's Parish – Glasgow Building Preservation Trust
St Andrew's RC Cathedral – Mon Gerald Sharkey
St Anne's RC – Fr Artur Stelmach
St Benedict's RC – Fr Jim Thomson
St Paul the Apostle – Fr David Brown
Triratna Buddhist Centre – Hilary 'Bear' Barclay

My apologies to anyone I may have missed.